101
Science Projects

Robert Hirschfeld

Troll Associates

Metric Conversion Chart

1 inch = 2.54 cm
1 foot = .305 m
1 yard = .914 m
1 mile = 1.61 km
1 square mile = 2.6 square km
1 fluid ounce = 29.573 ml
1 dry ounce = 28.35 g
1 ton = .91 metric ton
1 gallon = 3.79 l
1 pound = 0.45 kg
1 cup = .24 l
1 pint = .473 l
1 teaspoon = 4.93 ml
1 tablespoon = 14.78 ml

Conversion from Fahrenheit to
Celsius: subtract 32 and then
multiply the remainder by 5/9.

Interior Illustrations by Kathleen Kuchera

Copyright © 1994 by Troll Associates, Inc. All rights reserved.
Permission is hereby granted to the purchaser to reproduce,
in sufficient quantities to meet yearly student needs, pages bearing
the following statement: © 1994 by Troll Associates, Inc.

ISBN: 0-8167-3274-4

Printed in the United States of America.
10   9   8   7   6   5   4   3

Table of Contents

Introduction v

Plants

Come Out, Sprout!............................ 7
Plants from Seeds; Seeds from Plants/Some
    Fungus Among Us............................ 8
Flower Power 9
Name Those Parts! (Reproducible)..............10
Pores for Breath/Just Passing Through.......11

Animals

How You've Changed!...................12
The Story of Benny Beetle (Reproducible)......13
An Egg-speriment.................................14
Whale Wear 15
An Earthworm Knows—Without a Nose........16

The Human Body

As Simple as Breathing! 17
Gee, It's a Knee!...................................18
What Kind of Joint Is This? (Reproducible) 19
Sweat and Stay Cool 20
Let's Play Detective!................................21
Who Done It? (Reproducible)....................22

The Five Senses

Letting in the Light/Seeing Topsy-Turvy........23
Now You See It—Now You Don't! 24
The Right Touch....................................25
Follow Your Nose/.The Great Smell Escape ...26
Teaming Up to Taste 27
Right or Wrong? (Reproducible) 28
How Sound Gets Around/Making a Pitch 29

Food and Nutrition

Save Those Teeth!/Iron You Can Drink! 30
Getting a Rise....................................31
Fat Equals Energy/Take Your Vitamin C........32
Meet Miss Muffet...................................33
Spaghetti Art....................................34
Cooked or Raw? (Reproducible) 35

The Environment

Breathing Buddies/The Wrong Kind of Rain ..36
The Greenhouse Blues 37
Some Garbage Isn't Trash 38
Good Garbage? (Reproducible) 39
Designed for Desert Living.......................40

The Earth

Clay Contours 41
Build Your Own Island (Reproducible)...........42
The Layered Look 43
A Do-It-Yourself Volcano/Fire Rocks............44
Earth's Shaky Shell 45
Bath Towel Mountains..............................46
How Do Your Crystals Grow? 47
Fancy Formations 48
Which Formations Are Which?
    (Reproducible) 49

The Ocean

Putting on the Pressure 50
Icebergs Aren't Nice Bergs/An Amazing
    Pick-Up! 51
Salt Water Stunt/Puffed-Up Waves 52

Air and Water

Air Tips the Scales/Is Air Space an
     Empty Space? 53
Full of Hot Air/Amazing Air Pressure 54
Why Do They Fly? 55
Simple Siphon 56
Over the Top/Five Streams into One 57
Will It Float? 58
Detergent Makes a Difference 59

Weather

Winds Are Current Affairs 60
Quicker to Heat, Quicker to Cool/Jiminy
     Crickets! 61
Pop! Goes the Thermometer/What's the
     Humidity? Ask a Pine Cone! 62
Lightning in the Classroom 63
First Comes Lightning, Then Comes Thunder .64
How Far Away Is the Storm? (Reproducible) ..65

Color and Light

Hidden Colors 66
Mad Mirrors/"Breaking" a Spoon with
     Water 67
Bending Beams 68
Up Periscope! 69

Simple Machines

Weighing Work/Are You So Inclined? 70
Longer Distance Means Less Work
     (Reproducible) 71
Rolling Along on Ball Bearings/Wheels
     Need Axles 72
Here's to Gears! 73
Screws and You 74
Building Up Your Pull with Pulleys 75
Pushing Down to Lift Up 76

Chemistry

Which Liquid Has More Pull? 77
Layers in a Glass 78
Chemistry Heats Things Up 79
Moving Molecules/Funny Money 80
Cabbage Chemistry 81
Acid or Base? (Reproducible) 82
An Acid Test/Secret Messages 83
What's the Picture? (Reproducible) 84

Magnets

Magnets Are Choosy/A Field of Filings 85
Match Up the Magnets (Reproducible) 86
Poles Together, Poles Apart/The Giant
     Magnet 87
Are All Magnets Created Equal?/Breaking
     the Cardboard Barrier! 88

Space

Creating Craters 89
Safe Sunshine/Big Shadows, Little Shadows .90
Where's the Sun? (Reproducible) 91
What Turns on the Moonlight?/What
     Outshines the Moon? 92
Tilting Toward the Sun 93
The Temperature's Greater at the Equator 94
Different Angles/What We'd Weigh
     on Other Worlds 95

Bibliography

Suggested Resource Books on Specific
     Science Topics 96

INTRODUCTION

101 Science Projects brings you 101 ways to enrich your classroom with the excitement of hands-on science. With intriguing experiments that teach and test concepts from a wide sampling of science topics, you'll find fascinating ways to add to or extend any science unit or to motivate students to question and explore new topics that capture their interest.

The Activities

Each activity in the book not only demonstrates a specific science concept, but is designed to encourage students to think like scientists—questioning, predicting, testing, measuring, comparing, recording data, and drawing conclusions. Some of the experiments in **101 Science Projects** will seem incredible. But finding out that every one can be explained by sound scientific principles is one of the most important science lessons your students will ever learn. In addition, participating in the activities, obtaining results, and drawing conclusions will give students a sense of accomplishment, confidence, and success that will motivate learning across the curriculum.

The activities also provide plenty of opportunities for cooperative learning. In many you'll find suggested ways to organize students into groups, with special jobs for each group member.

All experiments in **101 Science Projects** have been tested either in the classroom or by the author. Each project is preceded by a list of materials you'll need—most found in the classroom or home and all inexpensive and easy to obtain. When necessary, sources for materials are suggested. All activities are safe for the elementary classroom, with special words of caution when a demonstration should be performed by the teacher or when extra adult supervision is advised.

Grade Levels

101 Science Projects is designed for use across a wide span of grade levels. You'll find some experiments especially geared for young learners, but most are adaptable for a range of ages. More advanced students will be able to do most of the activities themselves, while younger children will need more teacher involvement. Throughout the book you'll find a selection of reproducible activity sheets that reinforce the concepts taught or provide an opportunity to gather and record data. Many experiments also provide a particularly interesting scientific explanation for the results. Share these explanations with your more advanced students.

Most of all, **101 Science Projects** can turn your classroom into a living laboratory where students discover the fun and excitement of scientific discovery and gain a sense of wonder about the natural world as its secrets are revealed.

Come Out, Sprout!

- **CONCEPT:** A plant begins with a seed.

- **MATERIALS:** clear plastic glasses, blotting paper or paper towels, water, absorbent cotton, radish seeds (available from gardening supply stores), paper cups

Most young children know that plants come from seeds. But when seeds are planted in soil, the very first stages of growth occur where we can't see them. Explain that it is possible to start seeds growing without soil so that we can see the baby plants when they first start to emerge. (For mature plants to develop, the seedlings need to be transferred to soil.)

Divide the class into small groups. Give each group a clear plastic glass lined with a piece of blotting paper or paper towel almost to the height of the glass. Have students pour about an ounce of water into each glass and then fill the glass with absorbent cotton. Next, give each group a few seeds in a paper cup. Show students how to insert a few seeds between the paper and the side of the glass so the seeds are visible.

After two or three days, the seeds will begin to sprout. Point out the tiny roots and stems of the baby plants. Have children check the progress of their plants every day. Suggest that they draw pictures showing the changes they observe.

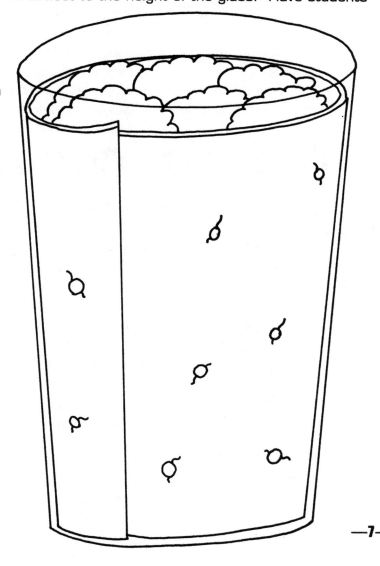

Plants from Seeds; Seeds from Plants

- **CONCEPT:** Plants make their own seeds.

- **MATERIALS:** fruits and vegetables (peppers, apples, cucumbers, melons, squash, tomatoes, etc.), magnifying glasses

- **PREPARATION:** Spread newspaper on work surfaces and slice open the fruits and vegetables for groups to examine.

Children know that plants grow from seeds. But where do seeds come from? Students will be interested to learn that seeds come from plants! The part of the plant that contains the seeds is called the *fruit*. In fact, some foods that we call vegetables, such as tomatoes, cucumbers, and peppers, are technically fruits.

Divide the class into groups and provide each with samples of cut fruits and vegetables. Point out the seeds, suggesting that students examine smaller seeds with magnifying glasses. Discuss the wide variety of shapes and colors that seeds come in, as well as the number of seeds different plants produce. Have students draw and label the seeds they find in the different fruits and vegetables they examine.

Some Fungus Among Us

- **CONCEPT:** Molds are plants that grow on food.

- **MATERIALS:** white bread, water, sandwich bags, magnifying glasses

Ask students if they have ever seen a slice of bread or piece of old food that got moldy. Tell them that mold is a type of fungus—a tiny plant that has no seeds.

Place slices of white bread and several drops of water in two sandwich bags and seal the bags. Keep one bag in a warm, dark place, and the other in a refrigerator. Have children check the bags after three days. What do they see? (The bread in the warmer bag will have dark patches, while the bread in the colder bag will not.) Explain that the dark patches are mold. The cold stopped the mold from growing on the refrigerated slice of bread. Let students examine the mold with magnifying glasses.

Flower Power

- **CONCEPT:** Different parts of flowers help make new seeds.

- **MATERIALS:** several large flowers, such as tulips, daffodils, lilies (available in flower shops); magnifying glasses; toothpicks

Explain that flowers have parts that enable plants to make their own seeds. Then divide the class into small groups and give each group a flower to work with. (Note that not all flowers have all the parts pictured in the diagram or described below.)

Have students carefully remove the *petals*, revealing the inner flower. Tell the class that the central tube is called the *pistil*. The slender stalks around the pistil are the *stamens*. Each stamen has a sac on top, the *anther*, which contains *pollen*. Instruct students to remove a stamen carefully and rub off some pollen to examine under a magnifying glass.

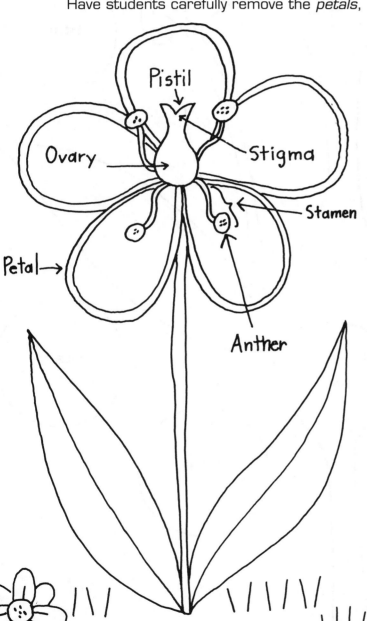

Invite the students to feel the top of the pistil. How does it feel? (sticky) This sticky part is the *stigma*. Explain that there is a tiny opening in the stigma leading to the *ovary* at the base of the pistil. Demonstrate how to brush a little pollen onto the stigma. (The pollen should stick to it.) Tell the class that the ovary contains the plant's *eggs*. Ask one student to split the pistil carefully with a toothpick. The eggs might be visible inside. (Lily eggs are especially visible.) If the pistil is difficult to split, assist children as needed.

Explain that for a plant's seeds to grow, the pollen grains must combine with the eggs. This is called *pollination,* which occurs when pollen blown by the wind or carried by bees or birds lands on the stigma. Once the seeds have been pollinated, the ovary grows and becomes the plant's *fruit*. The fruit protects the seeds and provides them with food.

Name_____ Date_____

Name Those Parts!

Can you name all the parts of a flower? Read the flower parts in the circles. Draw a line connecting each name to the correct part of the flower. Then color the flower. Use any colors you like.

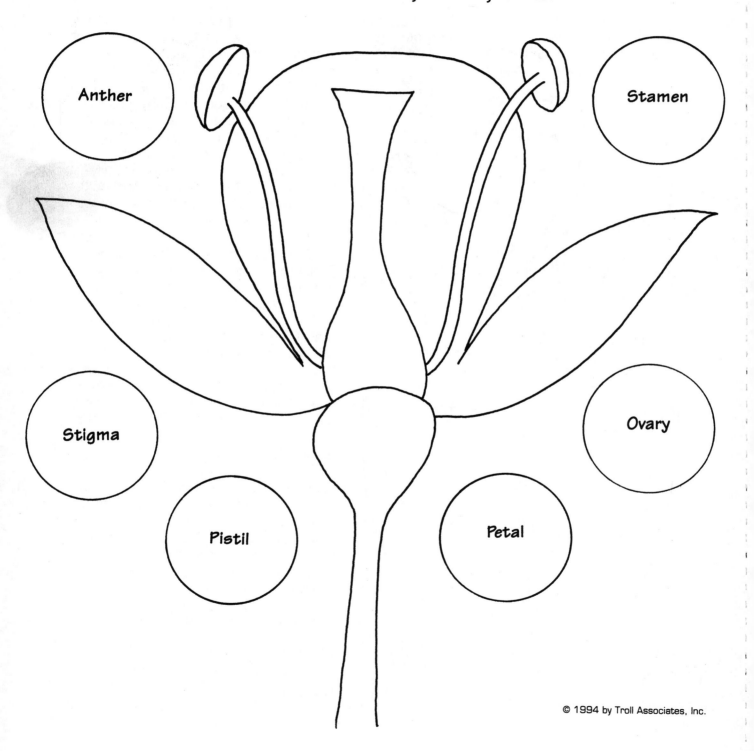

Anther

Stamen

Stigma

Ovary

Pistil

Petal

© 1994 by Troll Associates, Inc.

Pores for Breath

- **CONCEPT:** Plants "breathe" through their leaves.

- **MATERIALS:** a potted plant, petroleum jelly

Ask students if they think that plants, like animals, need air. Explain that leaves take in air through tiny invisible holes, or *pores*, in their leaves.

To prove this, ask a volunteer to completely coat one of the plant's leaves, top and bottom, with petroleum jelly. Explain that this will keep air from reaching the pores. In a week the coated leaf will have died. To discover more about leaf pores, have a student coat one leaf on the top only, while a second student coats another leaf on the bottom. The leaf coated on the bottom will die, but not the one coated on the top. Ask students to conclude whether the leaf pores are on the top or on the undersides of the leaves.

Just Passing Through

Before

- **CONCEPT:** Water enters the roots of a plant through tiny root hairs.

- **MATERIALS:** clear plastic glasses, water, raisins, a saucer

Divide the class into groups. Give each group a clear plastic glass of water and ten to twelve raisins. Tell students to place half the raisins in the water overnight. Have them leave the rest of the raisins on a saucer. What do children observe the next day? The dry raisins are unchanged, while those in the water have swelled. What caused this? Explain that water soaked through the skins of the raisins because water molecules are small enough to move through the walls of plant cells. The roots of a plant have tiny *root hairs* growing from them. The root hairs have very thin skins—thinner than the skin of a raisin. Water gets into the plant's root hairs and then into the roots the same way the water got into the raisins.

After

How You've Changed!

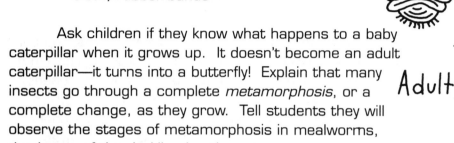
Eggs

Larva

- **CONCEPT:** An insect changes its appearance from one phase of its life cycle to another.

- **MATERIALS:** several dozen mealworms (inexpensive and easily obtained from pet stores that sell reptiles), magnifying glasses, large clear jars, flour (or bran or oatmeal), apples, nylon stockings or cheesecloth, rubber bands

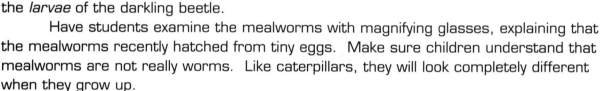
Pupa

Adult

Ask children if they know what happens to a baby caterpillar when it grows up. It doesn't become an adult caterpillar—it turns into a butterfly! Explain that many insects go through a complete *metamorphosis*, or a complete change, as they grow. Tell students they will observe the stages of metamorphosis in mealworms, the *larvae* of the darkling beetle.

Have students examine the mealworms with magnifying glasses, explaining that the mealworms recently hatched from tiny eggs. Make sure children understand that mealworms are not really worms. Like caterpillars, they will look completely different when they grow up.

Let children work in groups and give each group a jar. Instruct groups to fill each jar with flour, bran, or oatmeal, adding an apple slice to provide the mealworms with a source of liquid. Tell students to put some mealworms in each jar, cover the jar with nylon or cheesecloth, and secure the cover with a rubber band. Assign a child in each group to be responsible for changing the apple slice once a week.

Have students examine the jars with a magnifying glass from time to time. After a few weeks the larvae will appear lifeless. They are now in the *pupa* stage. After a few more weeks, adult beetles will emerge.

Encourage children to keep a log, drawing and/or describing the changes they observe and noting the date of each observation.

Name_____ Date_____

The Story of Benny Beetle

Read the story of Benny Beetle. Fill in the missing words by matching the pictures with the words at the bottom of the page.

Let me introduce myself. My name is Benny Beetle, and I am

an insect called a darkling beetle. But I didn't always look the way I do

now. At the very beginning of my life I was just a tiny _____ .

When I hatched I was a mealworm. But I wasn't really a worm. I

was a beetle _____ . I wiggled around and ate a lot.

Then, one day, I stopped eating. I stopped moving.

I looked like I was dead. But I wasn't. I was in my _____

stage. When I came out of my pupa case, I was all grown up.

That's how I got to be the_____ beetle I am today!

Use these words to fill in the blanks: pupa larva adult egg

© 1994 by Troll Associates, Inc.

An Egg-speriment

- **CONCEPT:** Chick or duck embryos can be seen inside an egg.

- **MATERIALS:** a cylindrical box (such as an oatmeal box), scissors, a desk lamp with a 100-watt light bulb, a few fertilized duck or chicken eggs

- **PREPARATION:** Contact your local 4-H Club for fertilized eggs. If you decide to hatch the eggs in class, the 4-H Club might also furnish an incubator, feed for the hatchlings, and necessary instructions. Afterwards, the club will probably adopt the baby birds.

Tell students that there is a way to see a chick or duck *embryo* inside an egg. Invite them to offer ideas for how this can be done without harming the baby bird in the egg. Then introduce the term *candling* and set up the following apparatus. (Older children will be able to set up the equipment with your help.)

Remove the bottom from a cylindrical cereal box. Cut a hole in the lid, smaller in diameter than the eggs. Now place the box over the unshaded light bulb and turn on the lamp.

To view what is happening inside the egg, hold it about two inches over the hole in the box. Warn students not to let the egg overheat, keeping it close to the light for only a short time. The chick or duck embryo should be visible through the shell. If no clear shape is evident, the embryo is probably still very young. Let children candle the egg each day. As the embryo develops, they will be able to see a more defined shape. Suggest that students record the embryo's development in a log, drawing and describing the changes each day.

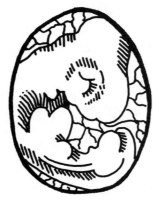
4 days

18 days

newly hatched

Whale Wear

- **CONCEPT:** Blubber keeps whales warm.

- **MATERIALS:** a large bowl of ice water, plastic bags, duct tape, a large plastic freezer bag, a pound of solid fat (margarine or vegetable shortening), rubber bands

Ask children why we need to wear heavy clothes in cold weather. How do animals like bears, dogs, or birds protect themselves against the cold? Discuss the fact that mammals and birds need to keep their body temperatures the same, even when the weather is cold. Fur and feathers help keep these animals warm. Snakes and fish don't need to keep warm because they are "cold-blooded." Tell the class that whales are not fish but mammals. How can warm-blooded mammals with no fur or feathers to keep them warm survive in icy cold waters? Explain that whales have a thick layer of fat, or *blubber*, under their skins. A whale's blubber keeps it warm.

To show how blubber helps keep whales warm, choose volunteers to put their bare hands in ice water. How long can they keep them there before they become too uncomfortable? Enlist helpers to record the length of time the volunteers keep their hands submerged. Next, give a student a small plastic bag to put on like a glove and

have a partner seal the bag around his or her wrist with tape. (The tape should touch the bag only.) Meanwhile, fill the larger freezer bag with shortening and knead it until it is soft. When ready, help the student place his or her covered hand inside the bag of fat, securing it with a rubber band. Have the student dip the fat-insulated hand into the bowl of ice water. Can he or she feel the cold? Compare the time a bare hand can remain in the ice water with the time a hand protected by a layer of fat can stay submerged. Let other students try the experiment. Conclude by explaining that the fat in the bag is like whale's blubber.

An Earthworm Knows—Without a Nose

- **CONCEPT:** Earthworms have a sense of smell.

- **MATERIALS:** earthworms (obtainable at bait shops or from the ground), paper towels, cotton balls, nail-polish remover, water

- **PREPARATION:** Moisten the paper towels with water.

Recall with children that the nose is the sense organ we use to detect odors. How about other animals? Dogs, cats, horses—all have noses, and all use their noses to sniff out odors. But what about animals that don't have any recognizable sense organ for the purpose of smelling? Do students think those animals can detect odors anyway? To find out, divide the class into groups and give each group a moistened paper towel with a few earthworms on it. Point out that earthworms are living creatures and must be handled carefully.

Inform students that the towels are wet because earthworms move better on a moist surface. Ask students if they can see noses on the worms. How can they find out if earthworms can detect odors even without noses?

Provide each group with two cotton balls. Tell students to wet one with nail-polish remover and the other with plain water. Ask a student in each group to hold the water-dampened cotton ball close to *but not touching* the worm. What happens? (There should be little or no response.) Have a second student do the same with the cotton ball moistened with nail-polish remover. What do the children predict will happen this time? The worm will react, recoiling from the strong smell. Suggest that students hold the cotton with the nail-polish remover close to different parts of the worm, such as the tail and the midsection. What happens? Wherever the cotton ball is placed, the worm will attempt to move away from the odor.

What conclusions can students draw from this experiment? Even though earthworms don't have visible sense organs, they do react to odors. Explain that every part of an earthworm's body is equally sensitive to smells. (After the activity, release the worms outdoors.)

As Simple as Breathing!

- **CONCEPT:** Our lungs expand when we breathe in and contract when we breathe out.

- **MATERIALS:** a clear plastic bottle, a large balloon, a small balloon, a plastic straw, a rubber band, modeling clay

- **PREPARATION:** Make a model lung for children to experiment with. First cut off the bottom of a clear plastic bottle. Also cut off the top of a large balloon, keeping the part with the stem. Knot the stem and place the open end over the bottom of the bottle. Then fasten the small balloon to the straw with a rubber band and insert it, balloon down, into the bottle. Seal the bottle neck with clay so that the only way air can get into or out of the bottle is through the protruding straw.

Tell students they will use a *model* to see what happens when we breathe. First challenge them to predict what will happen if they pull down on the balloon stem. Then give the model to a student to try. Children should see the balloon inside the bottle inflate. When the stem is pushed slightly into the bottle, the small balloon should deflate. Ask a volunteer to repeat pulling and pushing on the stem while students take turns placing a finger near the top of the straw. What do they feel? They should notice a flow of air coming from the straw when the bottom balloon is pushed up.

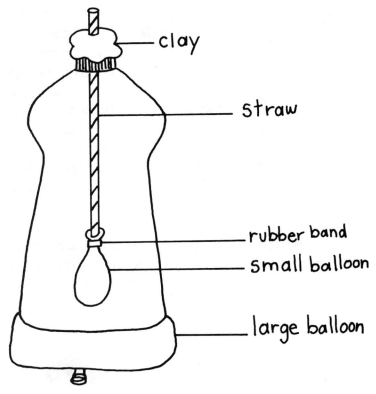

Explain that our lungs are similar to the small balloon. The bigger balloon is like the large muscle beneath our lungs (the *diaphragm*). When students pull down on the stem of the large balloon, air fills the small balloon. When we breathe in, our diaphragms move downward, making our lungs expand. When students push up on the large balloon, air is expelled from the small balloon. When we breathe out, our diaphragms move upward, making our lungs contract. Have students breathe in and out with their hands on the sides of their chests to feel their lungs get bigger and smaller as their diaphragms move down and up.

Gee, It's a Knee!

- **CONCEPT:** Our joints allow our bodies to move.

- **MATERIALS:** construction paper, tape, rubber bands, paper fasteners, hole punchers, old socks (optional)

Ask students which parts of their bodies they can move and make a list of the joints they name, such as elbows, wrists, fingers, knees, jaws. Tell students that they will create models of one of their joints—the knee—to learn how it moves.

Instruct each student to make one long tube by rolling a sheet of construction paper the long way, and then to make two short tubes by rolling two sheets of construction paper the short way. Show how to tape the tubes to hold their shape.

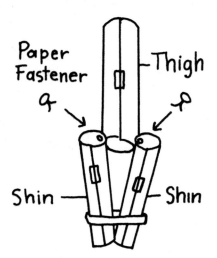

Explain that in the lower leg, there are two bones (the *tibia* and the *fibula*) and that in the upper leg (*thigh*), there is one longer, heavier bone (the *femur*). Show children how to arrange the paper tubes so that the two shorter ones, representing the shin bones, form a "V" into which the longer tube, representing the thigh bone, will fit.

Give each student a rubber band and two paper fasteners. Show how to punch two holes in the sides of the long tube as shown, about 3/4" from the end, and one hole in the side of each shorter tube. Line up the holes so each paper fastener can attach one of the shorter tubes to the longer tube as shown in the illustration. Hold the free ends of the shorter tubes, or "shin bones," together with the rubber band. Encourage students to experiment with their models to see how their legs bend at the knee. Remind them that, while the model knees can move in a complete circle, their *own* knees bend only one way. (For added realism—and a touch of humor—have children fit old socks over the "foot" ends of their models.)

Name_____ Date_____

What Kind of Joint Is This?

Find this child's ankle,
knee, shoulder, elbow,
and wrist joints.
Label each joint with its name.

© 1994 by Troll Associates, Inc.

Sweat and Stay Cool

- **CONCEPT:** Sweating helps to cool the body.

- **MATERIALS:** an outdoor or room thermometer, cotton balls, rubbing alcohol

Ask children what happens to their bodies when they play very hard, especially when it is very hot. When children mention *sweat*, ask if they have any ideas about why we sweat when we are hot. The following experiment will show that sweating has a purpose.

Place the thermometer on a table, leaving it there long enough to register the room temperature. Have a volunteer record the temperature on the chalkboard. Ask another student to soak a cotton ball in rubbing alcohol and partially cover the thermometer bulb with the wet cotton. Have a third volunteer blow across the cotton about fifteen times. Then pass the thermometer around for students to see that the temperature has dropped. Record the lower reading on the chalkboard.

Why do children think the reading on the thermometer changed? After they offer ideas, explain that blowing on the alcohol in the cotton caused the alcohol to *evaporate*, or turn from a *liquid* into a *vapor*. Because evaporation uses up heat, the alcohol absorbed heat from the mercury in the thermometer.

Further explain that when a person's body gets hot, small glands beneath the skin release fluid to the skin's surface. This fluid, or *sweat*, evaporates like the alcohol in the experiment. It absorbs heat from the skin, and as a result, the skin gets cooler, causing body temperature to lower.

Let's Play Detective!

- **CONCEPT**: No two people have exactly the same fingerprints.

- **MATERIALS**: pencils, blank white paper, transparent tape, index cards, magnifying glasses

Tell students that they are about to learn something that detectives are trained to do. Divide the class into groups of four. Provide each group with two index cards per child. Then instruct students on how to take their fingerprints:

1. Rub the sharpened end of a pencil over a sheet of blank white paper about twenty times to accumulate a layer of *graphite*.

2. Rub your index finger over the graphite.

3. Ask a partner to help you stick a piece of tape over the graphite on your finger.

4. Remove the tape and stick it on an index card.

5. Label the card with your name.

6. Make another fingerprint of the same finger on a second card, but don't put your name on it.

Tell group members to put the labeled cards in a pile and to each take one of the unlabeled cards. Challenge students to use magnifying glasses to examine the prints they are holding and match them with the prints on the other cards. What can children conclude from this experiment? Confirm that each person has her or his own unique fingerprint pattern.

Name_____ Date_____

Who Done It?

Somebody ate the last slice of chocolate cake and left chocolate fingerprints all over the plate! Can you figure out who it was? Each of the suspects is shown next to his or her fingerprint. Draw a circle around the chocolate-cake eater. Good luck!

© 1994 by Troll Associates, Inc.

Letting in the Light

- **CONCEPT:** Our eyes adjust to changing light.

- **MATERIALS:** an unshaded lamp

Pair off students and have them watch their partners' eyes when they look into the turned-on lamp. Then turn off the lamp. Ask students what they see. (The *pupil* of the eye gets smaller when light is bright and larger when light is dim.) Explain that the pupil is really a tiny hole that adjusts in size to let just enough (but not too much) light into the eye. Have children draw their partners' pupils as they looked in the bright and dim light.

Seeing Topsy-Turvy

- **CONCEPT:** Our brains "correct" what our eyes see.

- **MATERIALS:** a clear round glass bowl filled with water, an unshaded table lamp with a 200-watt bulb, a sharp pencil, a sheet of black construction paper, a piece of white cardboard with a glossy finish

Place the bowl of water on a table with the lamp about two feet away. Elevate the bowl on a stack of books so that it is level with the light bulb. With the sharp end of a pencil, make a round hole in the center of the black construction paper. Have a student hold the paper between the bowl and the lamp. Ask another student to hold the white cardboard on the other side of the bowl with the glossy side facing the bowl. Now dark-

en the room and turn on the lamp. Instruct the student to move the white cardboard closer to or farther from the bowl until an image of the bulb appears on it—upside down!

Explain that our eyes work in the same way. The hole in the black paper is like the pupil of the eye, and the white sheet is like the back of the eye, or *retina*. The image the eye sends to the brain is upside down like the one on the white cardboard, but the brain automatically corrects the eye's mistake!

Now You See It—Now You Don't!

- **CONCEPT:** Our eyes have blind spots.

- **MATERIALS:** index cards, black markers or crayons, rulers

Give an index card to each student. Have each child draw a heavy black dot on his or her card, then a small X four inches to the right of the dot.

Each child should hold the card at arm's length with the dot lined up with his or her right eye and the left eye closed. As children move their cards *slowly* toward them the X will suddenly disappear! If they continue moving their cards closer the X will reappear.

Next, have students close their right eyes and repeat the process, this time lining up the X with their left eyes. The dot will vanish and then reappear. Can students explain why this happens?

Explain that every eye has a tiny *blind spot* where the *optic nerve*, the communication line between the eye and the brain, enters the eye. The back of the eye, the *retina*, is covered with cells that are sensitive to light, but at that one spot the optic nerve gets in the way. When an object (the X) is lined up with the blind spot, it seems to vanish. When the object moves out of the blind spot, it comes back into view. We don't usually notice objects "disappearing" because our brains "fill in" for our blind spots.

The Right Touch

● **CONCEPT**: Some parts of our bodies are more sensitive to touch than others.

● **MATERIALS**: pencils, masking tape

Ask students to name parts of their bodies that can feel things. Which parts do they use most often to find out how something feels? Have students run their hands over things around them: their desks, their clothing, their faces, their hair. Challenge them to come up with descriptive terms for how things feel and make a list on the chalk-board: *hard, soft, smooth, rough, warm, cool, sharp, pointy, curved, flat,* and so on. Inform youngsters that a network of nerve endings all through the skin responds to dif-

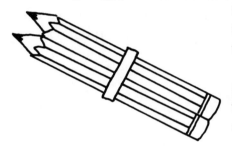

ferent sensations and sends messages to the brain about the temperature, the texture, and the shape of things we touch.

Divide the class into pairs and give each pair three pencils. Help children tape two pencils together, so that the points are even with each other. Tell one partner in each pair to close her or his eyes.

Give the students the following instructions:

1. While your partner has his or her eyes closed, lightly touch the inside of your part-ner's forearm with either the two pencil points taped together or the single pencil point, but don't tell which. (Be gentle—don't poke!)
2. Ask your partner whether he or she felt one point or two points. Try it a few more times, writing down how many right and wrong answers your partner gives.
3. Now *gently* touch the tip of the your partner's finger or thumb with the two taped pencils or the single pencil point. Can he or she tell the difference between one point or two this time?
4. Switch places and try the experi-ment again.

Explain that the fingertips have many more nerve endings than other parts of the body. Elsewhere on the body the nerve endings are too widely scattered to register the touch of two pencil points close together.

Follow Your Nose

- **CONCEPT:** Our sense of smell can help us to find objects.

- **MATERIALS:** cotton balls, perfume, pine-scented room deodorizer

Saturate one cotton ball with perfume and one with room deodorizer. Tell two children to close their eyes while you dab a little of each scent onto several well-separated objects in the room. Provide each volunteer with one of the cotton balls to use as a sample and challenge children to sniff out the objects that match the scents. Suggest that the rest of the class give clues whether the sniffers are getting "hotter" or "colder." Repeat the activity with other volunteers, pointing out that people can track by smell just as dogs can—only not nearly as well!

The Great Smell Escape

- **CONCEPT:** Smells can pass through some materials.

- **MATERIALS:** vanilla extract, an eye dropper, a small balloon

Let children smell the closed bottle of vanilla. Can they tell what the liquid smells like? Open the bottle and let them smell the vanilla extract. Using an eye dropper, drip three or four drops of vanilla extract into the balloon, making sure that none touches the outside. Partially inflate the balloon and knot it closed. Do students think they will be able to smell the vanilla through the rubber? (They will be able to detect a faint odor.)

Why can we smell the vanilla through the balloon but not through the bottle? While the balloon *appears* solid, there are microscopic holes in the rubber that let the vanilla molecules through. Glass, however, is not *porous* like rubber.

Teaming Up to Taste

- **CONCEPT:** The senses of sight, smell, and taste work together.

- **MATERIALS:** a raw potato, an onion, an apple, a cucumber, a carrot, grapes, a vegetable peeler, a knife, paper plates, blindfolds

- **PREPARATION:** Peel the vegetables and fruits, slice them, and arrange the slices on several paper plates so that each plate has some of each fruit and vegetable.

Ask students which they would rather taste—the raw potato or the apple. The apple should win by a landslide. Do children think they could taste the difference between the two without seeing or smelling?

Blindfold a volunteer and give her or him one slice of apple and one of potato. By tasting them, can the student identify which is the apple? Repeat the test with the volunteer holding his or her nose. Conclude that without the sense of smell it is hard to distinguish between the two tastes. Have another blindfolded volunteer taste a piece of apple or potato, but this time while sniffing an onion. What does the food taste like now? [The food sampled should taste like onion.] What does this experiment prove? Confirm that the powerful onion odor sends a stronger message to the brain than that sent by the weaker tastes of the apple and potato, so the brain is fooled.

Divide the class into groups. Let them experiment with different combinations of fruits and vegetables, discovering to what extent the sense of taste depends on sight and smell. Give each group a copy of the chart on page 28 to record the number of times a blindfolded group member makes a correct identification and the number of times he or she is fooled.

Further explain that the nerve endings on the tongue can detect only a few tastes: sweet, sour, salty, bitter. Other distinctions in taste come from our sense of smell. Also, when we see what we're about to taste we anticipate what the flavor is likely to be.

Name_____ Date_____

Right or Wrong?

Foods	Holding Nose		Sniffing Onion		Sense of Smell Working as Usual	
Apple or potato?	right	wrong	right	wrong	right	wrong
Apple or cucumber?	right	wrong	right	wrong	right	wrong
Apple or carrot?	right	wrong	right	wrong	right	wrong
Potato or cucumber?	right	wrong	right	wrong	right	wrong
Potato or carrot?	right	wrong	right	wrong	right	wrong
Carrot or cucumber?	right	wrong	right	wrong	right	wrong

© 1994 by Troll Associates, Inc.

How Sound Gets Around

- **CONCEPT:** Sound vibrations reach our ears more effectively through a solid conductor than through air.

- **MATERIALS:** metal spoons, 24" lengths of string

Divide the class into groups, giving each group a spoon with the handle tied to the exact middle of the string. Have one member of each group be the experimenter. Instruct one student to help the experimenter wrap one end of the string around his or her left index finger and the other end around the right. Tell the experimenter to let the spoon swing freely as a group member taps it with another spoon. What kind of sound do the children hear? Next have the experimenter hold an index finger in each ear while a group member again taps the spoon. To the experimenter, the sound will have a deeper pitch. Explain that when the sound vibrations travel up the string directly to the listener's ears they are much stronger than when they are dispersed into the air.

Making a Pitch

- **CONCEPT:** Faster vibrations create higher-pitched sounds.

- **MATERIALS:** glasses or jars of the same size, water, metal spoons, a xylophone

Let children work in small groups. For each group fill three glasses or jars with different amounts of water and let students experiment by hitting the jars with a metal spoon to hear which glass makes the highest-pitched sound (the one with the most water).

Let students strike different bars on the xylophone. The shorter bars make a higher-pitched sound. Help students figure out that the water in the glass stops the vibrations, leaving a shorter length of glass to vibrate. The shorter the object struck, the faster the vibrations. Faster vibrations make higher-pitched sounds.

Save Those Teeth!

- **CONCEPT**: The acid in carbonated cola drinks is bad for teeth.

- **MATERIALS**: chicken bones, clear plastic glasses, carbonated cola

Most children have heard that cola drinks are bad for teeth. Can students think of a way to find out if this is really true—without actually endangering their teeth? Explain that teeth and bone are made out of similar substances—both contain *calcium*. Cola drinks contain *acid*. To see what the acid in a cola drink can do to teeth, instruct groups of students to observe what happens when they leave a chicken bone to soak in a glass of cola for a week. Much of the bone will be dissolved!

Iron You Can Drink!

- **CONCEPT**: There is iron in some food.

- **MATERIALS**: tablespoons, four kinds of juice (pineapple, apple, cranberry, and white grape), clear plastic glasses, strong tea

Most children have heard that our bodies need iron. Does food really contain iron? To prove that it does, give students four glasses. Instruct students to put four tablespoons of each juice in separate glasses and label the glasses. Then have them add four tablespoons of strong tea to each glass, stir, and let the mixtures stand for twenty minutes. Dark particles of iron will appear at the bottom of the pineapple juice. After two more hours, particles will be visible in the grape juice and cranberry juice. None will appear in the apple juice. A chemical reaction with the tea separates the iron from the three juices. The more iron, the quicker the reaction. Which juice contains the most iron? (pineapple) Which contains none? (apple)

Getting a Rise

- **CONCEPT**: Yeast gives off carbon dioxide when mixed with warm water and sugar.

- **MATERIALS**: a measuring cup, warm water, a tablespoon, sugar, a packet of dry yeast, a funnel, a small balloon

Ask children if they've ever watched bread bake. Did they wonder why the dough rises? What causes it to rise? The following experiment will help them understand how *yeast* makes bread rise.

Ask a student to help you add a tablespoonful of sugar and the contents of a yeast packet to a cupful of *warm*—not hot—water. As the yeast dissolves, children will be able to observe bubbles forming on the surface of the water. What makes the bubbles? Explain that the yeast is giving off some sort of gas.

To explore further, insert the neck of a funnel into the neck of the balloon. Ask a student to pour the yeast mixture through the funnel into the balloon and knot the balloon closed. Store the balloon in a warm place. If yeast makes bubbles, what do students predict will happen to the balloon?

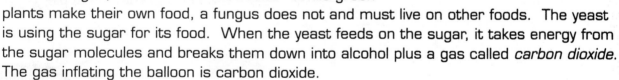

Have the class check the balloon for changes every five minutes or so. After an hour the balloon will be noticeably inflated. Explain that while yeast looks just like a powder, it is actually a living thing—a type of plant called a *fungus*, related to a mushroom. While green plants make their own food, a fungus does not and must live on other foods. The yeast is using the sugar for its food. When the yeast feeds on the sugar, it takes energy from the sugar molecules and breaks them down into alcohol plus a gas called *carbon dioxide*. The gas inflating the balloon is carbon dioxide.

The yeast in bread dough feeds on sugar, and the escaping carbon dioxide "blows up" the dough, causing it to rise. These bubbles form the little air holes that we see in baked bread. The mouth-watering smell of baking bread comes from the yeast. Consider baking bread with the class as a follow-up to this experiment.

Fat Equals Energy

- **CONCEPT**: Fat is a source of energy.

- **MATERIALS**: straight pins, a shelled cashew nut, a shallow metal pan, a match

Stick three pins into the nut and use the resulting tripod to stand the nut in a pan. Ask students to predict how many seconds the nut will burn if lit with a match. Then use a match to set fire to the nut. Explain that the fat in the nut—in the form of oil—burns. The flame will last quite a while because fat stores so much heat energy. Fat performs the same function in our bodies, storing up energy we need to grow and be active. *This experiment should be done only as a demonstration by an adult.*

In a follow-up discussion remind children that while some fat is important in our diets, a little goes a long way. Too much fat in our diets isn't healthy.

Take Your Vitamin C

- **CONCEPT**: Vitamin C prevents oxidation.

- **MATERIALS**: a cup of water, a shallow dish, vitamin C tablets, an apple, a knife, a lemon

Pour about a cup of water into the shallow dish and dissolve four or five vitamin C tablets in the water. Cut apple wedges for students to soak in the solution. Students will observe that an untreated apple wedge browns, or *oxidizes*, faster than the ones soaked in the vitamin C solution. Vitamin C helps prevent oxidation.

Tell the group that many fruits contain vitamin C. How can we tell which ones? Try the same experiment with lemon juice. (Mention that oranges and grapefruits are also high in vitamin C content.)

Meet Miss Muffet

- **CONCEPT**: Milk can be separated into solid and liquid parts.

- **MATERIALS**: whole milk, small jars (as from baby food), paper cups, clear vinegar

- **PREPARATION**: For each group, put two tablespoons of vinegar into a paper cup.

Have children recite "Little Miss Muffet" together. Do they know what "curds and whey" really are? Tell them they will find out by making curds and whey themselves.

Provide each small group with a jar almost filled with fresh whole milk and a paper cup of vinegar. Tell students to pour the vinegar into the milk, close the jars, and shake up the mixture. Wait three minutes, then ask children to examine the jars to see what has happened. The milk will have separated into two parts, one that is solid and white and the other that is clear and liquid. Tell students that the solid part is called *curds* and the liquid part is called *whey*.

Explain to the class that milk is made up of tiny solid particles that are *suspended*, or floating, in liquid. When vinegar, an acid, is added to the milk, it causes the tiny solid particles to form clumps, or *curds*. The tiny solid particles also give milk its color. Therefore the remaining liquid, or *whey*, is clear.

Point out that the curds and whey Miss Muffet was eating did not contain any vinegar. *That* mixture would probably be enough to frighten anyone away, even without a spider!

Spaghetti Art

- **CONCEPT**: Cooking changes the texture of foods.

- **MATERIALS**: uncooked spaghetti, a hot plate or stove, a cooking pot of water, oven mitts, a colander, paper plates

- **PREPARATION**: Boil a pot of water. Make sure students are kept well away from the heat source and boiling water.

Ask students to name some favorite foods they eat raw (some fruits or vegetables, perhaps). What are their favorite cooked foods?

Let the class work in pairs. Give each pair several strands of uncooked spaghetti. Can children break the strands into pieces and make shapes, numbers, or letters with them? Can they make an H?... a 1?... a triangle? What about a Q, a 3, or a circle? Challenge students to figure out how they could make curved shapes with spaghetti.

Now cook some spaghetti. Remove the cooked spaghetti, drain, and set it aside to cool. Make sure the spaghetti is quite cool before putting a few strands on a paper plate for each pair of children. Invite students to experiment, making different shapes, letters, and numbers. What has happened to the spaghetti to make it easier to work with? Cooking changed the spaghetti, making it soft and flexible. Ask the class to name other foods that change when cooked. What about eggs? Meats? Vegetables? How do they change?

Name_____ Date_____

Cooked or Raw?

Some foods have to be cooked. Some you can eat without any cooking at all. For each picture, circle the C if the food has to be cooked. Circle the R if you can eat it raw. Circle both letters if you can eat the food cooked or raw.

C   R   C   R

C   R   C   R

© 1994 by Troll Associates, Inc.

We're in this together.

Breathing Buddies

- **CONCEPT**: Animals and plants help each other breathe.

- **MATERIALS**: a glass bowl, aquarium gravel, heavy-duty plastic from a trash bag, freshwater aquarium plants, goldfish, goldfish food

Have children help prepare a classroom aquarium. Rinse the bowl and gravel with clear, cold water. Spread gravel on the bottom of the bowl and put plastic over it to keep it in place. Fill the bowl with fresh, cold water, remove the plastic, and set the plants in the gravel. After one day put in the fish. Feed the fish and add water as needed, *always* letting water stand for 24 hours before adding. Encourage the class to observe the fish, and point out that although the fish breathe oxygen from the water, the oxygen never runs out. Why?

Explain that green plants, such as those in the bowl, give off oxygen, which fish (and all other animals) need to breathe. Fish, like other animals, breathe in the oxygen and breathe out carbon dioxide, which plants need to survive.

The Wrong Kind of Rain

- **CONCEPT**: Acid rain is harmful to plants.

- **MATERIALS**: two potted plants, quart jars with lids, water, vinegar, a measuring cup

Explain that motor exhaust and other industrial wastes in the air pollute the rain, creating *acid rain*. What do students think this does to plants?

Have children fill two quart jars with tap water and add a cup of vinegar to one. (Recall with children that vinegar is an acid.) Every few days, have students water one plant with clean water and the other with the acid solution. After a week children should notice that the plant watered with "acid rain" is much less healthy. Explain that acid rain has a similar effect on our food crops.

Acid Rain

Clean Water

The Greenhouse Blues

- **CONCEPT**: The earth is warmed by the *greenhouse effect*.

- **MATERIALS**: outdoor or room thermometers, clear plastic bags

- **PREPARATION**: This activity requires a sunny day. Each group needs windowsill space in direct sunlight for ten minutes.

Ask if children have ever been inside a greenhouse. Tell them that this activity shows how greenhouses help plants grow. It also demonstrates an important environmental problem called the *greenhouse effect*.

Arrange students into groups and distribute to each group two thermometers and a clear plastic bag. Ask the groups to put one thermometer in the bag, leave the other one out, and place both on the windowsill in direct sunlight. After ten minutes, ask students to record the temperatures of both thermometers. Why do the thermometers in the bags register higher temperatures?

Explain that because the plastic bags are transparent, sunlight passes through them easily. Inside the bag, sunlight converts to heat, which cannot get out as easily as the light got in. A greenhouse works the same way, letting sunlight in through the glass and trapping the heat inside.

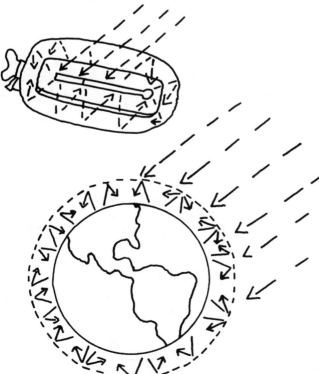

In the same manner, sunlight passes through the atmosphere that surrounds our planet. The heat from the sun cannot get out as easily as the light got in. The trapped heat raises the temperature. We call this phenomenon the *greenhouse effect*.

Inform students that some scientists believe that the increased burning of fuels for transportation and industry is raising the level of carbon dioxide in the atmosphere. Consequently, too much heat is being trapped by Earth's atmosphere. What effect could overall higher temperatures have on our environment? Challenge students to suggest solutions to this problem.

Some Garbage Isn't Trash

- **CONCEPT:** Some garbage is biodegradable.

- **MATERIALS:** clay flowerpots, gravel, soil, garbage items (clean vegetable scraps, grass clippings, paper, clean Styrofoam cups or fast-food packages, plastic bags, foil), water, glass pie plates, newspaper, sticks

- **PREPARATION:** This experiment involves several weeks' observation, so avoid using any materials that will be unpleasant or potentially dangerous to have in the classroom for a long time.

Give each child a flowerpot with gravel in the bottom (to keep it from leaking). Help children fill the pots about a third with soil. Tell them to add a layer of clean garbage items broken up into small pieces. Then have them put in more soil until the pot is nearly full. As they work, explain that a lot of our garbage is disposed of this way— in open spaces called *landfills*, where garbage is covered over with soil.

Have children add a little water to the pots. Mark the pots with the students' names, cover them with glass pie plates, and put them in a warm, dark place. Challenge students to predict what will happen to the garbage in the miniature landfills they have made. Make sure children check their pots periodically, adding water if the soil is dry. After four weeks, have students empty their pots onto sheets of newspaper. Have them use sticks to spread out and examine the contents. They should find some of the garbage, such as Styrofoam, foil, and plastic, unchanged. But the *organic* garbage, such as food and plants, will have begun to turn to soil. Ask students to tell you why garbage that is *biodegradable* (turns back into soil) is better for the environment than garbage that takes many, many years to *decompose*.

Name_____ Date_____

Good Garbage?

The trash can marked GOOD is for biodegradable garbage. The trash can marked BAD is for garbage that does not decompose. Draw a line from each piece of garbage to the can it should go into.

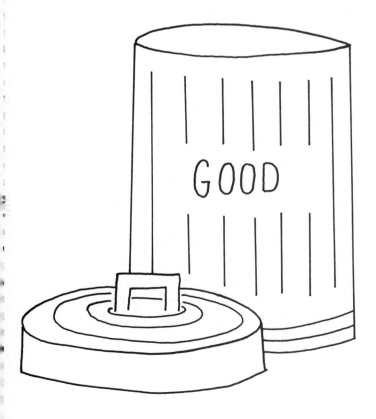 

GOOD   BAD

© 1994 by Troll Associates, Inc.

Designed for Desert Living

- **CONCEPT**: Cacti are well adapted to the dry conditions of the desert.

- **MATERIALS**: a real cactus (if available) or pictures of cacti, three paper towels, water, newspaper, a cookie sheet, wax paper, paper clips

Invite children to share their impressions of the desert. Ask if they know why camels are so well adapted to desert life. (They can go for days or even months without water.) Then explain that desert plants are also well adapted for life with little water.

Show students a cactus plant or pictures of cacti. Ask them to compare the leaves of a cactus plant with those of a tree or flower. Tell students that both the thickness and rounded shape of the cactus leaf help it to save water. Another feature that helps cacti survive in the desert is a waxy coating.

Dampen three paper towels (wet, but not dripping). Give a volunteer one towel to lay flat on a newspaper-lined cookie sheet. Ask another student to roll the second into a cylinder and place it on the cookie sheet beside the first. Show a third child how to roll up the remaining paper towel and wrap it in wax paper, fastening the wax paper in place with paper clips. Place the wax-paper roll beside the other two. Set the cookie sheet with the three paper rolls in direct sunlight and leave it for about two hours.

Ask the students if they think the towels are still wet. On examination, they should find that the flat paper towel will be dry. The rolled, uncovered paper towel, while dry outside, will be damp inside when unrolled. The towel wrapped in wax paper will be dampest of all.

Challenge students to explain these results. Confirm that the water in the flat towel evaporated fastest because the whole towel was exposed to the air. The inside of the rolled, uncovered towel stayed damp because it was protected from the air. The wax paper stopped water evaporation almost completely in the covered towel.

Similarly, the thick, round shape of a cactus slows down evaporation because the inner part of the cactus is protected from the air. The waxy coating of the cactus also keeps water inside the plant. As a result, a cactus can live a long time without rain.

Clay Contours

- **CONCEPT**: A *contour map* shows the shape of a landscape.

- **MATERIALS**: any ordinary map, clay,
  plastic knives, paper, pencils, copies of page 42

Show the class an ordinary map, asking what the map tells about the area it represents. (Most maps show the two-dimensional shape of landforms.) What doesn't the map show? Can students tell where there are hills, mountains, and valleys? (The map may use symbols or colors to indicate whether the landscape is flat or mountainous, but it doesn't show three-dimensional details.) Explain that geographers use a special kind of map called a *contour* map to indicate what the contour, or shape, of a landscape really looks like. Have students make their own contour maps.

Provide children with clay and instruct them each to build a small clay "mountain." Show them how to slice a piece off the top of the mountain and trace the shape onto a sheet of paper as shown. Have students do the same with a second slice placed over the outline of the first. As they slice off and trace more pieces, the outlines of the slices will get larger. Point out that the concentric outlines form a *contour* map of the clay mountain.

Distribute copies of the contour map on page 42. Again, provide children with clay and ask them to roll out ropes of clay, flattening one "rope" around contour 1, two around contour 2, and so on until the children have "built" the island represented on the map. Explain that on real contour maps, each contour line would be marked with a number showing the height (in feet or meters) of the landform at that point.

As a follow-up activity, suggest that students build a clay model of a familiar area and draw a contour map that shows the features of the landscape.

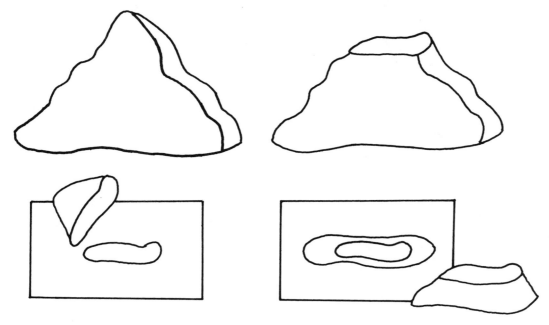

Name _____Date _____

Build Your Own Island

Roll out long ropes of clay. Lay one rope around section 1 on the contour map. Flatten it out to cover all the space between the lines. Use two thicknesses of clay for section 2, three for section 3, and four for section 4. Now you can see the landscape of your island.

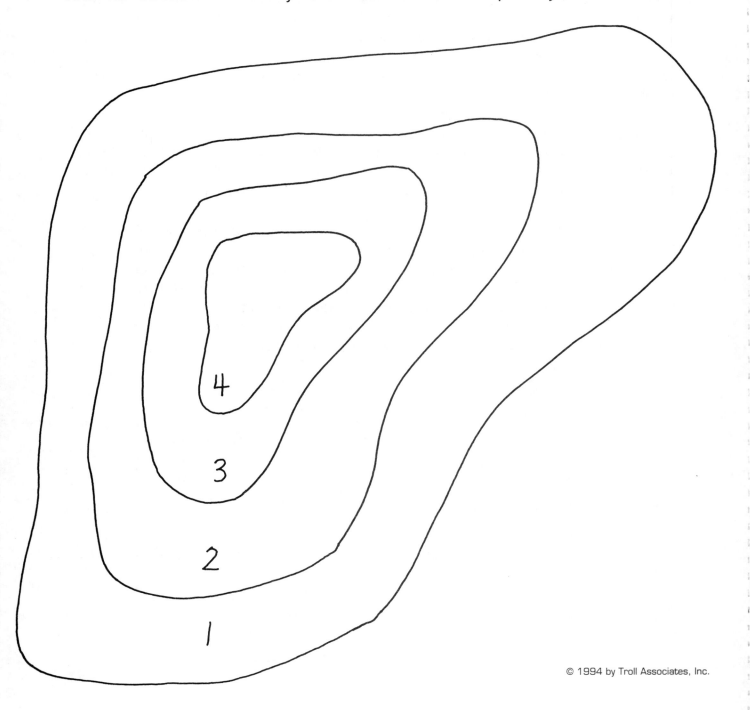

© 1994 by Troll Associates, Inc.

The Layered Look

- **CONCEPT**: The earth is made of layers of different materials.

- **MATERIALS**: wide-mouth jars, aluminum foil, zip-lock bags, water, clay (hardening type), modeling clay, cardboard, scissors, black crayons or markers, soil, pebbles

Explain that we can make models that show what scientists believe is inside the earth.

Give a jar to each group of students. Tell group members to crumple up aluminum foil in the bottom of the jar. This represents the earth's *inner core*. Explain that the inner core is made of solid iron and nickel that is so hot it glows white. Use a sealed zip-lock bag with a little water inside to represent the hot melted iron and nickel of the *outer core*. These two sections combined are as big as the entire moon!

Next, tell the students that above the core is the earth's *mantle*, which is divided into three parts. The *deep mantle* is made of solid rock. Have the children use clay that will harden to represent the deep mantle. The next part is called the *asthenosphere*. It is made of semi-solid rock that can flow at a very slow rate. Have children use modeling clay to represent the asthenosphere. They can use more hardening-type clay to represent the solid *upper mantle*, which lies above the asthenosphere.

The uppermost layer is the earth's *crust*—a hard, black layer of solid rock. The crust can be represented by a cardboard circle cut to fit the jar and colored black. Let students sprinkle a layer of soil and pebbles on top of the cardboard, explaining that soil covers the earth's crust. The class may be surprised to learn that more of the earth is covered by water than by land.

Make sure students understand that the earth is round like a globe. The model they've created represents the layers of the globe from the inside out.

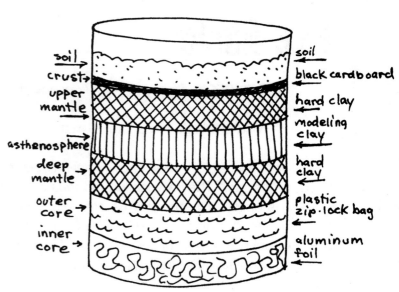

A Do-It-Yourself Volcano

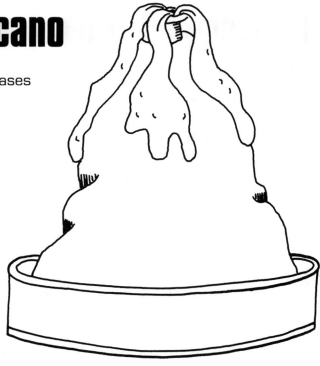

- **CONCEPT**: Expansion of heated gases causes volcanoes to erupt.

- **MATERIALS**: a baking pan, a small soda bottle, moist soil or sand, a funnel, a tablespoon, baking soda, a measuring cup, vinegar, red food coloring

Place the bottle in the pan. Instruct children to create a "mountain" by piling soil or sand around the bottle up to the opening. Place the funnel into the bottle and have a student pour in a tablespoon of baking soda. Have another child stir red food coloring into a cup of vinegar. Ask a third student to pour the vinegar into the bottle. A red froth will erupt from the mouth and flow down the "mountain."

Explain that the vinegar reacts with the baking soda to form carbon dioxide gas, building up pressure and forcing the liquid from the bottle. Similarly, volcanoes erupt when gases deep inside the earth heat and expand. The pressure eventually forces molten rock (*magma*) from deep in the earth to flow out of the mouth of the volcano and down the sides as *lava*.

Fire Rocks

- **CONCEPT**: *Igneous rock* is created when a volcano erupts.

- **MATERIALS**: a candle, a match, a cup of cold water

Ask students if they know where rocks come from. Explain that some rocks come from volcanoes. They are called *igneous rocks,* which means "fire rocks."

As children watch from a safe distance, light the candle and let the melted wax drip into the cup of cold water. The cold water will make the wax solidify. Tell the children to feel the bits of hardened wax. Can they explain why the liquid wax turned to a solid? (It cooled.) Similarly, the *lava* that comes out of a volcano turns to solid rock as it cools.

Earth's Shaky Shell

- **CONCEPT**: The earth's crust is made of moving plates.

- **MATERIALS**: enough pudding mix to provide a snack for the class, the other ingredients listed on the pudding mix box, a saucepan, a hot plate or stove, an oven mitt, a large spoon, a cake pan, plastic wrap, graham crackers, paper cups, plastic spoons

Ask students the following riddle: "How is the earth like a bowl of chocolate pudding?" They will find out after this science activity.

Make the pudding, keeping children a safe distance from the hot plate. Pour the hot liquid pudding into the cake pan and cover it with plastic wrap. Once the pudding cools, carefully remove the plastic wrap so that the "skin" of the pudding comes off with it.

Tell the class that the earth's outer shell is solid rock, but deeper down is a layer of rock similar in consistency to chocolate pudding that has cooled. (If students have done the activity on page 43, explain that the solid outer shell is called the *lithosphere* and is made up the earth's *crust* and *upper mantle*. The semi-solid layer beneath is the *asthenosphere*.)

Help volunteers place graham crackers on top of the pudding. Explain that the earth's outer shell sits on a layer of semi-solid rock just as the crackers sit on the pudding. Also like the crackers, the earth's outer shell is made up of sections. Scientists call these sections *plates*. Let students move the crackers on top of the pudding to get an idea of how the earth's plates move on the semi-solid layer beneath.

Discuss with children why we aren't aware of the movement of the earth's plates, explaining that it is the same reason that we don't see the movement of a clock's hour and minute hands—the movement is too slow to be noticed. Can students guess what happens when the plates move suddenly or break apart? (An earthquake occurs.)

Once the experiment is finished, spoon the pudding into cups for children to enjoy. While they are eating, see if they can answer the riddle you posed at the beginning of the activity.

Bath Towel Mountains

- **CONCEPT:** Some mountains are formed by the force of the earth's plates pushing together.

- **MATERIALS:** bath towels, books

- **PREPARATION:** Ask children to bring bath towels to class.

This experiment may be performed in conjunction with the previous one, in which students learned that the earth's outer shell is made up of moving *plates*. The "plate" concept is central to understanding the formation of mountains.

Discuss with the class that while the earth is basically round like a globe, it is definitely not smooth like most globes. Ask students what kinds of formations make the surface of the earth uneven. Guide them to name hills and mountains, valleys and canyons, for example. Do children have any ideas about why our planet has mountains instead of a smooth surface?

Divide the class into groups and provide each with a bath towel and two books. Recall with students that rather than being a single intact unit, the surface layer of the earth is broken up into separate sections, or *plates*. These plates are in constant motion because they rest on a layer of semi-solid rock. Explain that sometimes a plate will be pushed in by plates on either side.

Ask one student in each group to fold a bath towel in quarters and lay it on a table. Explain that this represents a plate of the earth's outer shell. Have two other group members place a book on opposite ends of the towel. Explain that the books also represent plates. Have the students slowly push their books toward each other. What happens to the towel? The surface of the towel will fold upward.

Just as the towel folded upward when pushed from the sides by the books, a plate will also fold upward when pressure is applied by plates on both sides. Because the process is like folding, geologists call the resulting formations *fold mountains*.

Make sure the students understand that this process is so slow that we are not aware of it. The earth's plates move so slowly that it takes millions of years for a mountain to form.

How Do Your Crystals Grow?

- **CONCEPT**: Crystals form when water evaporates from a saturated solution.

- **MATERIALS**: rough stones or brick fragments, glass baking dishes, table salt, measuring cups, tablespoons, hot water, Epsom salts, ammonia, magnifying glasses

We know that animals and plants grow, but how about rocks? In a sense, many rocks can be said to "grow," too—through a process called *crystallization*. Some of the most beautiful formations in nature are crystals. Tell students that they will get to watch crystals develop and grow over several days.

Divide the class into groups, instructing each group to carefully spread stones or brick fragments in two baking dishes. Tell students to stir table salt into half a cup of hot water until no more will dissolve. Then have them add another tablespoon of salt, stir, and pour the salt solution over the bricks or stones in one dish.

For the other dish, help the groups mix a cup of Epsom salts, a cup of hot water, and three tablespoons of ammonia. *[Handle the ammonia carefully so that students do not inhale the fumes. Either add it yourself or supervise closely.]* Pour this mixture into the second dish. Label the dishes with the type of solution and the names of all group members. Put them where they can remain undisturbed.

After about two days, crystals will begin to grow as the water evaporates. Have students observe the crystals with the aid of magnifying glasses, noticing the differing forms the crystals in each dish take. Suggest that they draw pictures of the crystals to show the differences in form. Explain to the class that many rocks are formed by this process over long periods of time.

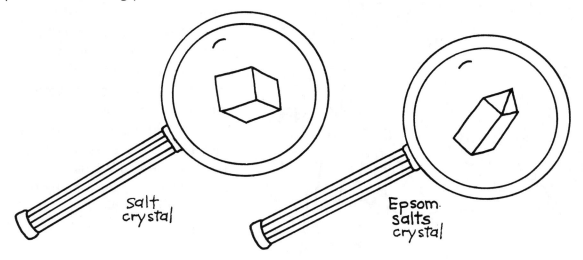

salt crystal

Epsom salts crystal

Fancy Formations

- **CONCEPT**: Stalactites and stalagmites are formed when water carrying dissolved minerals drips from the roof of a cave.

- **MATERIALS**: pictures of cave interiors showing stalactites and stalagmites, shoe-box lids, clear plastic glasses, hot water, Epsom salts, food coloring, stirring spoons, long nails, string, magnifying glasses (Inexpensive poster-size photographs of the interiors of the Carlsbad Caverns are available by mail from: Carlsbad Caverns—Guadalupe Mountain Association, P.O. Box 1417, Carlsbad, NM 88221-1417, phone: 505-785-2318. Or you might try your local travel agent for brochures.)

Share with students that *spelunkers* are people who explore caves. Remind them that exploring caves should be done only by experienced adults. Show the class pictures of cave interiors and point out the beautiful rock formations. Explain that the formations that hang from the roof of a cave are *stalactites*, while the ones that grow up from the floor are *stalagmites*. Tell the class that water carrying tiny bits of dissolved rock drips from the ceiling of a cave. When the water evaporates, the dissolved rock begins to solidify.

Instruct each group of students to place a shoe-box lid, open side up, on a table and to set a glass inside each end of the lid. Have them fill the glasses with hot water, adding Epsom salts a little at a time until there is slightly more than will dissolve in the water. Have them add some food coloring to the water and stir.

Help each group tie each end of three lengths of string to a nail. Show how to drop one nail into each glass so that the strings are suspended between the glasses, hanging at least two inches below the rims of the glasses as shown.

Within one or two days the strings will become saturated and water will begin to drip onto the box lid. As the water evaporates, the salts will become solid, hanging from the strings like stalactites and building up on the lids like stalagmites. Allow the formations to grow for a full week.

We made some of those, too!

Name_____ Date_____

Which Formations Are Which?

Look at this picture of a cave. Do you see the stalactites and the stalagmites? Which are which? Color all the stalactites red. Color all
the stalagmites blue.

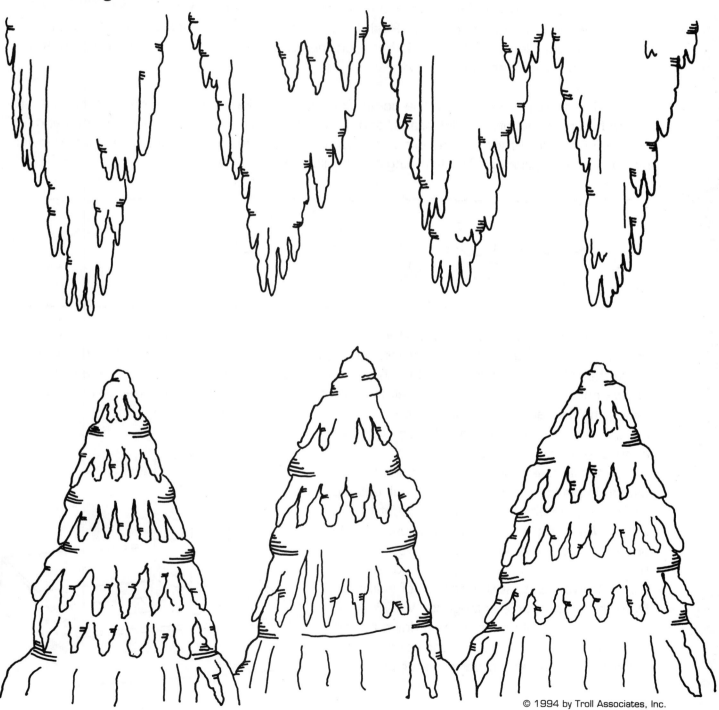

© 1994 by Troll Associates, Inc.

Putting on the Pressure

- **CONCEPT:** Water pressure increases as depth increases.

- **MATERIALS:** one-quart milk cartons, same-size nails, rectangular baking pans, rulers, empty cottage-cheese or margarine tubs, containers of water

- **PREPARATION:** Prepare one milk carton for each group of students. Open the whole top of each carton. Push three nails through one side of each carton in a vertical line with at least 1" between the nails. The lowest nail must be at least 3" from the base of the carton.

Share with students that the ocean floor isn't flat like a table. As on dry land, the ocean has high mountains, flat areas, and deep valleys. The living conditions for fish and other ocean animals vary at the different depths. For example, the water pressure at lower depths is much greater. The following activity illustrates why this is true.

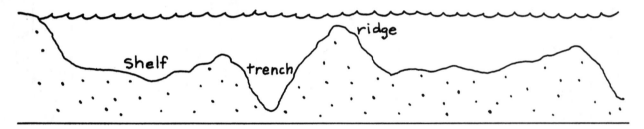

Distribute to each group of students a baking pan, a ruler, an empty cottage-cheese or margarine tub, a container of water, and a prepared milk carton. Instruct students to place the ruler in the baking pan lengthwise. Tell them to turn the cottage-cheese container upside down at the 1" end and to set the milk carton on top of the container with the nails facing the 12" end of the ruler (see illustration). Have students fill the milk cartons almost to the top with water.

While one group member holds the carton in place, instruct others to pull out the three nails simultaneously on the count of three. As water jets out of the holes, another student must keep pouring more water into the carton to keep the water level constant. Students will see that the stream of water from the bottom hole is longest. Why? A greater amount of water pushes down as the depth increases. So, too, in the ocean greater depth means greater water pressure.

Icebergs Aren't Nice Bergs

- **CONCEPT**: Most of an iceberg is below the surface of the water.

- **MATERIALS**: clear plastic glasses, water, ice cubes

iceberg

Invite children to offer definitions of an iceberg. Confirm that icebergs are chunks of ice that break loose from glaciers and drift in Arctic and Antarctic ocean waters. Why do students think they might be dangerous to ships? Let the class work in groups to find out. Give each group a glass filled with water. Have students drop in an ice cube. Lead them to observe that only the top of the cube is visible above the surface, with most of the cube not visible *under* the surface. Draw an iceberg on the chalkboard. Point out how the invisible, underwater part may stick out beyond the visible part. Now can they understand how it might endanger a ship?

An Amazing Pick-Up!

- **CONCEPT:** Salt water has a lower melting point than fresh water.

- **MATERIALS:** ice cubes, a clear bowl, very cold water, toothpicks, table salt

Float two ice cubes in a bowl of cold water and challenge students to think of a way to pick them up with a toothpick. Let them try. Then place one toothpick on each cube and have a student sprinkle a little table salt around one of the toothpicks. After two minutes invite a student to try picking up the unsalted ice cube using the toothpick as a handle. The toothpick will not pick up the ice. The toothpick on the salted ice cube, however, will.

Explain that salt lowers the freezing point of fresh water. Salting the ice made it start to melt, but the water froze again and trapped the toothpick.

Salt Water Stunt

- **CONCEPT**: Salt water is more *buoyant* than fresh water.

- **MATERIALS**: wide-mouthed jars, water, salt, stirring spoons, fresh raw eggs

Have one child fill a wide-mouthed jar with water and stir in salt until no more will dissolve. Then ask another child to *carefully* fill the jar halfway with fresh water, demonstrating how to pour it slowly onto a spoon held against the side of the glass so it doesn't mix with the salt water (see illustration). Now let a third volunteer gently lower an egg into the water. Students should notice the egg sinking through the fresh water but floating on the surface of the salt water! Explain that salt water is denser than fresh water and therefore more *buoyant*. The egg is denser than the fresh water and won't float on it, but it is *less* dense than the salt water, on which it does float.

Puffed-Up Waves

- **CONCEPT**: Wind is one cause of waves.

- **MATERIALS**: a fish tank, water, a large towel, straws

Do children have any ideas about where waves come from? Try this demonstration to find out. Put a fish tank on a towel to absorb spills and fill it almost to the top with water. Ask a student to blow gently across the surface of the water while the rest of the class observes. What do they see? (little waves) Let another student blow harder; the waves will grow bigger. Perhaps two or three students might blow across the water together. Let them try the experiment blowing through straws.

Conclude with the class that wind is one cause of waves. Of course, ocean waves are much bigger!

Air Tips the Scales

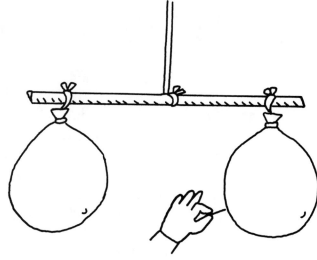

- **CONCEPT**: Air has weight.

- **MATERIALS**: two identical balloons, a yardstick, string, a needle

Does air weigh anything? Invite children to suggest a way to use balloons to find out. Inflate two balloons to the same size. Help students tie the balloons to the ends of a yardstick. Have one child tie a length of string to the middle of the yardstick and adjust until the yardstick hangs in perfect balance. What do children think will happen if one of the balloons pops? Puncture one balloon. The yardstick will tilt toward the inflated balloon. Why does this happen? (The air-filled balloon is now heavier.) Does air have weight? How can we tell?

Is Air Space an Empty Space?

- **CONCEPT**: Air takes up space.

- **MATERIALS**: clear plastic bottles, funnels, modeling clay, water

Does air take up space? Here's proof that it does. Divide the class into groups, giving each a plastic bottle, a funnel, and a ball of modeling clay. Have a student from each group put the funnel into the bottle and seal the gap between the bottle mouth and the funnel with clay. Make sure that the clay seals are tight. Ask students what they think will happen when water is poured into the funnel. Will it flow into the bottle? Let children try. The water stays in the funnel! Can students figure out what keeps the water from flowing into the bottle?

Explain that the bottle isn't really empty. It is full of air, leaving no room for the water.

AIR

Full of Hot Air

- **CONCEPT**: Hot air expands.

- **MATERIALS**: a plastic bottle, a balloon, a heavy saucepan, water, a stove or hot plate, ice water

Ask a student to fit a deflated balloon over the mouth of a plastic bottle and place the bottle in a saucepan of water. Place the saucepan on a stove or hot plate and heat the water. Be sure to keep children well away from heat source. Soon the balloon will begin to inflate. Ask students why they think this happens. Explain that the hot water heats the air in the bottle. As air warms, it expands. The air needs space to expand and the only space available is in the balloon.

What do children think might happen when the air cools? Can they think of a way to find out? Pour the hot water out of the saucepan and have a student replace it with ice water. The air will cool and the balloon will deflate.

Amazing Air Pressure

- **CONCEPT**: Air pressure pushes up as well as down.

- **MATERIALS**: a basin, a smooth-rimmed glass, water, a postcard or smooth cardboard that covers the mouth of the glass completely

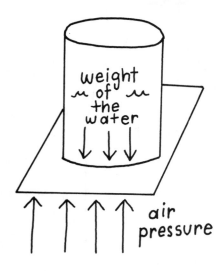

Conduct this activity over a basin to catch any spills. Have a child wet the rim of a smooth-rimmed glass, and fill it *to the brim* with water. Instruct the student to put a postcard or piece of smooth cardboard over the top of the glass, covering it completely. Help the child turn the glass over, keeping the postcard in place. Ask what will happen when the student takes his or her hand away from the card. The card will stay put, holding the water in the glass. Explain that the pressure of the air outside the glass pushes *up* on the card and is greater than the weight of the water pushing *down*. Let other children try.

Why Do They Fly?

- **CONCEPT**: Moving air exerts less pressure than still air.

- **MATERIALS**: a sheet of facial tissue for each student

Ask children if they've ever wondered how something as big and heavy as an airplane can fly. Have the class do this simple experiment to show what keeps airplanes up in the air.

Give each student a sheet of facial tissue. Show how to hold it horizontally with both hands and blow across the top of the paper. The result is unexpected: rather than hanging down, the outer end of the paper rises! The harder the children blow, the more the end of the tissue goes up.

Why do children think this happens? Explain that the faster air moves, the less pressure it exerts. The air being blown *over* the top of the tissue is moving faster than the air underneath. Therefore, there is less air pressure above than below. The greater pressure below pushes the tissue up.

But air moves both over and under an airplane wing. What keeps the airplane up? An airplane wing has a curved upper surface and a flat lower surface. Draw a diagram on the chalkboard similar to the illustration below. Explain that as an airplane flies, the air going over the upper, curved surface has to travel a greater distance than the air going under the flat, lower surface. Therefore, the air going over the wing has to move faster than the air moving underneath. The slower-moving air beneath the wing exerts more pressure than the faster-moving air above the wing. *Since the air pressure pushing up is greater than the air pressure pushing down, the airplane stays in the sky!*

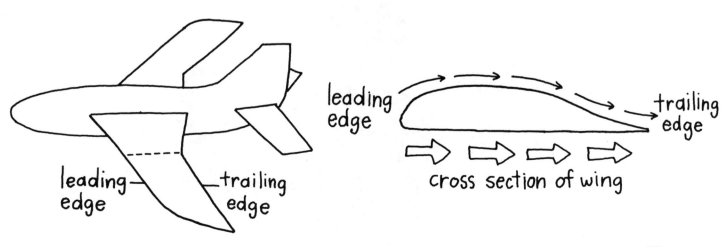

leading edge

trailing edge

leading edge

trailing edge

cross section of wing

Simple Siphon

- **CONCEPT**: Air pressure can make water move upward.

- **MATERIALS**: a basin, books, two large clear jars, water, food coloring, a one-foot or greater length of flexible clear plastic tubing (available in hardware or aquarium supply stores)

- **PREPARATION**: Place a basin of water on a table. Stack several books on the table as well. Fill a clear jar about two-thirds full of colored water. Place the jar on the stack of books and set an empty jar on the table top next to it. The stack of books should be high enough so that the bottom of the jar of water is higher than the top of the empty jar.

Present students with this puzzle: How can they transfer the water from one jar to the other without moving the jars? They might have a few ideas—an eyedropper, a straw, a spoon or ladle. Tell them there is a much quicker way. Submerge a length of clear plastic tubing into the basin so that the tube is completely filled with water. Put a finger over both ends of the tube to keep all the water in and remove the tube from the basin. Submerge one end of the tube in the full jar, keeping your finger securely over the other end so that no water runs out. Put the other end of the tube into the empty jar and take away your finger. At once, water from the upper jar will move upward through the tube and then down into the lower jar.

To go through the tube, the water had to move *upward* at first, defying the law of gravity. It did so because air pressure was pushing down against the water in the upper jar, forcing the water into the tube. Tell the class that when a tube is used like this it is called a *siphon*. After showing how the siphon works, let children try it themselves. By raising and lowering the two jars while the siphon remains filled, students can change the direction of the water flow.

Over the Top

- **CONCEPT**: Water has *surface tension*.

- **MATERIALS**: clear plastic glasses, pennies, water

Give each group of students a glass and eight to ten pennies. Fill the glasses to the brim with water and ask the students to predict how many pennies they can drop into the glasses without spilling any water. Let them take turns sliding coins, one at a time and edge first, into the glasses. As coins are added, the water rises noticeably *above* the edge of the glass. Explain that a property of water called *surface tension* gives liquids a kind of "skin." This surface tension keeps the water in the glasses from spilling.

Five Streams into One

- **CONCEPT**: Surface tension can join separate streams of water.

- **MATERIALS**: a coffee can, a hammer, a nail, running water

- **PREPARATION**: Use a hammer and nail to make five holes about 1/4" apart in a horizontal row near the bottom of an empty coffee can.

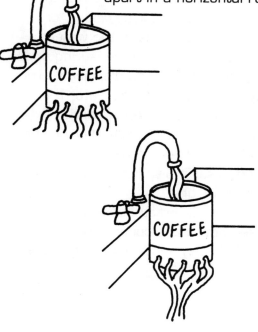

Share with the class this demonstration of surface tension at work. Hold the prepared coffee can under running water in a sink. Children will see that the water flows out of each hole in five separate streams. Ask a volunteer to try to "pinch" the streams together with a thumb and forefinger below the coffee can. The five streams will combine into one. Even when the student removes her or his hand, the single stream will remain held in place by surface tension. Ask if there's a way to divide the single stream into five once more. Have a student brush his or her fingers across the holes. The surface tension will be broken and the streams will separate.

Will It Float?

It sinks.   It floats.

- **CONCEPT**: Whether or not an object will float depends on the amount of water it displaces.

- **MATERIALS**: a large clear container, water, coins, modeling clay, basins, a clear plastic glass, two measuring cups

Fill the container with water and place it where all can see. Ask children if they think a coin will float or sink. Have a child drop a coin into the water to prove that it sinks. Do the same with a ball of modeling clay. Can students explain why these objects sink? Some may say the reason is that they are heavier than water. Now pose this question to the class: "Why will a small piece of metal (like a coin) sink in water but a huge metal ship will float?" Can the students think of a way to find out why?

Divide the class into groups, giving each a basin of water and each group member a ball of modeling clay. Ask children to shape their clay into little boats with the sides high enough to keep out the water. Then have students see if their boats will float. Why did the clay float when it was shaped like a boat, but not when it was shaped like a ball?

To find out, fill a clear plastic glass all the way to the top and place it inside a measuring cup. Let a volunteer drop a ball of clay into the water. Remove the glass to see how much spilled water is in the measuring cup. Now fill the glass again, set it in the other measuring cup, and repeat the procedure with a clay boat. Ask students to compare the amounts of water in the two measuring cups. (There is more in the first.)

Explain that when an object is placed in water, it *displaces*, or pushes aside, some of the water. The water in the two measuring cups is the water that was displaced. The clay boat displaced less water than the clay ball, even though both weighed the same. Whether or not an object will float depends on how much water it displaces—not on how much it weighs.

Finally, let students experiment to see how many coins they can put into their clay boats before they sink.

A metal ship floats.

But a metal anchor sinks!

Detergent Makes a Difference

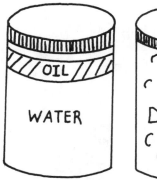 

- **CONCEPT**: Detergents cause insoluble substances to mix with water.

- **MATERIALS**: two dishes, vegetable oil, a basin, water, liquid detergent, clear jars with lids, talcum powder

Ask if children ever help wash dishes after meals. What do their families use to clean the dishes? Plan a test to see which cleans dishes better—water and detergent or just plain water. Spread some oil on each dish. Wash one in plain water and the other in water and detergent. Let children feel the dishes to see which feels cleaner.

Now divide the class into groups. Have each group partly fill a clear jar with water, add some vegetable oil, put the lid on the jar, and shake it. Students will see that the oil does not mix with the water but remains in a separate layer. Next, ask students to add just a few drops of liquid detergent and shake again. This time the oil will mix with the water to form a uniform, cloudy liquid.

Why do children think this happens? Explain that the detergent breaks up the oil into tiny droplets that will then mix with water. Detergent does the same thing to grease on dishes and pots. It breaks up the grease and makes it easier to clean away.

Here's another way to show how detergent works with water. Have students pour some water into a basin and sprinkle talcum powder on the surface of the water. They will find that the talcum powder does not mix with the water, but floats on the surface. What do children think might happen if they add some detergent? Have a student drop a little detergent into the basin. Now the talcum powder grains move toward the sides of the basin and then sink to the bottom.

Explain that talcum powder grains don't mix with plain water—they float on the surface because of surface tension. But the detergent coats the grains of powder, breaking the surface tension and sending the talcum powder to the bottom of the basin.

Winds Are Current Affairs

- **CONCEPT**: Winds are caused by the movement of warm and cold air.

- **MATERIALS**: a sheet of black construction paper, masking tape, an unshaded lamp, talcum powder

Challenge children to offer ideas about what causes wind. Explain that when air is heated, it rises. Colder, heavier air rushes in underneath. This rushing colder air is what we call *wind*. Can students think of any way to show how this happens?

Ask volunteers to tape a sheet of black construction paper to a wall or bulletin board. Place an unshaded lamp in front of the black paper and plug it in. Do not turn on the lamp yet.

Tell a student to hold a container of talcum powder above the black paper background and to sprinkle a little powder in front of the black paper. The class should see the grains of powder drift slowly downward. Now turn on the lamp. Allow a few minutes for the bulb to heat the air around it. Let children hold their hands near the light bulb (without touching it) to feel the air becoming warmer. What do students think will happen if talcum powder is sprinkled into the warmed air? Ask a child to sprinkle powder over the lamp. This time the grains of powder drift upward! Why do children think this happened?

Inform students that the heated air became lighter and rose upward, carrying the grains of powder with it. At the same time, cooler (and heavier) air rushed in to take its place. We can't feel the rush of cooler air in this experiment because the upward motion of the warmer air isn't strong enough. But greater differences in temperature between cool and warm air create much stronger air movements, or *currents*, resulting in wind. Very strong currents lead to cyclones, tornadoes, and hurricanes. Gentler currents might lead to a windy day for flying a kite.

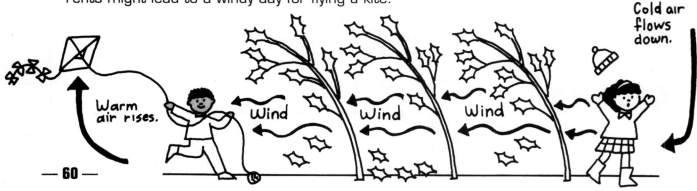

Quicker to Heat, Quicker to Cool

- **CONCEPT**: Land heats up and cools off faster than water.

- **MATERIALS**: a basin of topsoil, a basin of water, two outdoor or room thermometers

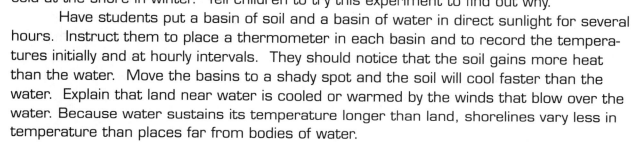

Ask children if they have ever noticed that in summer it isn't as hot at the beach as it is farther inland. Similarly, the weather doesn't get as cold at the shore in winter. Tell children to try this experiment to find out why.

Have students put a basin of soil and a basin of water in direct sunlight for several hours. Instruct them to place a thermometer in each basin and to record the temperatures initially and at hourly intervals. They should notice that the soil gains more heat than the water. Move the basins to a shady spot and the soil will cool faster than the water. Explain that land near water is cooled or warmed by the winds that blow over the water. Because water sustains its temperature longer than land, shorelines vary less in temperature than places far from bodies of water.

Jiminy Crickets!

- **CONCEPT**: We can guess the temperature by counting cricket chirps.

- **MATERIALS**: a cricket (can be obtained at pet shops), a jar, a nylon stocking, a rubber band, a watch with a second hand

A cricket can help us guess the temperature. Put a cricket in a jar and cover the mouth with a piece of nylon stocking held in place by a rubber band. Have a student count the chirps during fifteen seconds. Add forty to that number and you have the approximate temperature (in Fahrenheit)! Can students figure out why crickets chirp faster when it's warm? Confirm that crickets, being insects, are cold-blooded. Cold-blooded animals are more active when it's warm, and more sluggish when it's chilly. Slower movements conserve energy, so crickets chirp less in the cold. (Release the cricket when you've finished.)

Pop! Goes the Thermometer

There she blows.

- **CONCEPT**: A thermometer shows the temperature because liquid expands when heated.

- **MATERIALS**: small soda bottles, water, food coloring, clear plastic straws, modeling clay, a saucepan, a stove or hot plate

Have students working in groups fill a small soda bottle with colored water. Demonstrate how to put a straw halfway into the bottle and how to seal the bottleneck around the straw tightly with modeling clay. Instruct the groups to take turns placing their bottles into a saucepan of water heated on a stove or hot plate. What do students predict will happen? They will see the colored water rise in the straw as the water heats. Explain that liquids expand when heated and contract when cooled. Mercury is a liquid metal. When it is heated, it expands and rises inside the thermometer.

What's the Humidity? Ask a Pine Cone!

- **CONCEPT**: Pine cones react to changes in humidity.

- **MATERIALS**: paper cups, modeling clay, pine cones, straight pins, straws

Have students stick a little modeling clay on the bottom of an inverted paper cup. Push the base of a pine cone into the clay to hold the pine cone upright. Help children stick a pin straight into one of the scales of the pine cone and place a straw over the pin (as shown in the illustration). Now set the pine cone outside. When rain is imminent, the outer scales of a pine cone absorb moisture from the air, swell up, and close to protect the seeds inside. This makes the straw point upward. When the weather is dry, the cone opens, moving the straw outward at an angle. Challenge the class to try predicting rain using a pine-cone weather station.

Lightning in the Classroom

- **CONCEPT**: Lightning is a product of static electricity.

- **MATERIALS**: inflated balloons, articles of woolen clothing

- **PREPARATION:** This activity is best done when humidity is low. The day before, tell the children to bring in articles of clothing made of wool.

Invite children to share their impressions of thunderstorms. Do they think thunder and lightning are exciting? Scary? What do they think causes thunder and lightning?

Tell students that they might be able to make a little lightning right in the classroom. It will be completely safe because the lightning they produce won't be enough to cause damage or injury. Pair off the students and give each pair an inflated balloon. Have one partner in each pair rub the balloon rapidly ten times against woolen clothing. Darken the room as much as you can and let the children touch their balloons to metal objects in the room. They should see sparks between the balloons and the metal. Also, if they are very quiet, they may hear a faint crackling noise. Switch partners so everyone has a chance to try to make "lightning." Explain that the flash and crackle were caused by *static electricity*. Static electricity is caused by rubbing things together, which creates an *electrical charge*.

Explain that real lightning is also produced by static electricity. Strong air currents blow millions of ice crystals and water droplets together. They rub against each other, building up huge electrical charges. Finally, a gigantic spark leaps from the sky toward the earth. The spark is much more powerful than the tiny ones created in the classroom, but the principle is the same.

What about the thunder? The electricity from lightning heats the surrounding air so much, and the air expands so fast, that an explosion occurs. Thunder is the sound of that explosion. The little crackle students may have heard when they made their own lightning was mini-thunder!

First Comes Lightning, Then Comes Thunder

● **CONCEPT**: The difference between the speed of light and the speed of sound lets us calculate the distance of a storm.

If you live in an area where thunderstorms occur, ask students if they have ever noticed that they usually see the lightning *before* they hear the thunder. (If you don't have thunderstorms in your area, tell the class that this is the case.) Does anyone know why this happens?

Explain that light moves much faster than sound. If students can understand large numbers, inform them that light travels at about 186,000 miles per second! Sound is a real slowpoke, moving at only about 1,100 feet per second. So when lightning strikes, we see the flash almost as it happens. But the sound of thunder takes time to reach our ears. In fact, the difference between the speed of light and the speed of sound gives us a way to figure out how far away a storm may be.

Tell children that when they see a flash of lightning, they should start counting off seconds (by using either a second hand on a watch or one of the old standbys—"one Mississippi, two Mississippi, etc."); then stop counting when they hear the thunder. The number of seconds between the lightning and the thunder divided by five tells how many miles away the storm is.

Practice this with the class. Flick the room lights quickly, off-on-off, to simulate the lightning and then clap your hands or drop a book on the floor to represent the thunder. Have the class count off the number of seconds between the two and divide the resulting number by five. The class will know how far away the lightning would have been —if there had really been a storm, that is!

Name_____ Date_____

How Far Away Is the Storm?

Try these thunder-and-lightning word problems:

If there are ten seconds between a lightning flash and a clap of thunder, how many miles away is the storm? _____

If there are twenty seconds between a lightning flash and a clap of thunder, how many miles away is the storm? _____

If a storm is three miles away, how many seconds will there be between the lightning flash and the thunder? _____

If a storm is five miles away, how many seconds will there be between the lightning flash and the thunder? _____

© 1994 by Troll Associates, Inc.

Hidden Colors

- **CONCEPT**: Secondary colors are made up of different primary colors mixed together.

- **MATERIALS**: paints, paper cups, stirrers, paper coffee filters, scissors, markers (red, yellow, blue, orange, green, and brown), spring-type clothespins, clear plastic glasses, water

Discuss with students what they know about mixing colors or let them experiment, mixing red, blue, and yellow paints together to see what colors result. Can they mix other colors to make red, blue, or yellow? Explain that red, yellow, and blue are *primary colors*. All other colors are made by mixing two or more of these three.

Divide the class into groups and distribute materials. Each group should have a coffee filter, a pair of scissors, markers in each of the six colors listed above, six clothespins, and two glasses with a little water in each. Ask students to cut the filter paper into six strips, about $\frac{3}{4}$" wide. Have them use the markers to draw one circle of color *near* but *slightly above* one end of each paper strip.

Use clothespins to fasten the strips with the red, blue, and yellow circles to the inside of the glass so the bottom edge of each strip just touches the water, but the circle

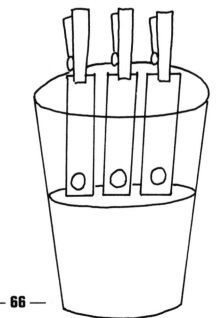

does not. As the filter paper absorbs water, the water will travel upward, reach each circle, and take some of the color with it. What colors do children see spreading up the paper? (red, blue, and yellow) What do they think will happen with the other three strips? Have them fasten the remaining strips to the inside of the other glass in the same fashion.

This time, as the water climbs up the paper strips, children will see the colors separating. Green will separate into blue and yellow. Yellow will separate from the orange color. And blue and orange will separate from the brown.

Conclude with children that the primary colors red, blue, and yellow combine to create *secondary* colors.

Mad Mirrors

- **CONCEPT**: Curved or uneven surfaces distort reflections by bending light.

- **MATERIALS**: large spoons (serving spoons or ladles), index cards, aluminum foil, scissors, glue

Distribute some large spoons to the students and have them study their reflections on both sides. On the *convex* (outward-curving) side, their reflections will be distorted; on the *concave* (inward-curving) side, they'll be distorted and upside down! To further experiment, let children create their own mini-funhouse mirrors. Have each student glue foil, shiny side up, onto an index card. Because the foil isn't perfectly smooth, the resulting reflections will be slightly distorted. By bending the foil into convex and concave shapes, even funnier reflections will appear. Explain that curved or uneven mirrors bend the light they reflect, bending the reflections as well.

"Breaking" a Spoon with Water

- **CONCEPT**: Water bends light.

- **MATERIALS**: straight-sided clear glasses, water, spoons

As students watch, place a spoon in a glass half full of water. Set the glass on a level surface with the water line at the students' eye levels. What seems to have happened to the spoon? It looks like it's broken! Remove the spoon from the water—it's straight again! Invite children to offer ideas about why this happened. Explain that the spoon looked broken in the glass because water bends light. Let students suggest other objects to "break"—a pencil, a straw, a ruler, and so on. Let partners or groups try experimenting on their own.

Bending Beams

- **CONCEPT**: Lenses bend light rays.

- **MATERIALS**: a sheet of cardboard, scissors, a comb, tape, a sheet of white paper, a flashlight, a magnifying glass, a pair of (old) prescription glasses from someone who is near-sighted

- **PREPARATION**: This experiment is best done in a darkened room.

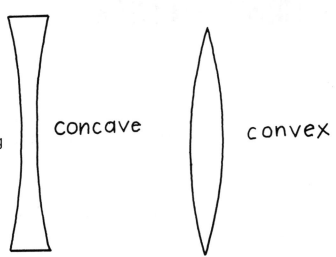

Encourage children who wear glasses to share with the class why they need them. Do their glasses help them see far away or up close? Explain that eyeglasses help correct vision because the glass isn't just plain and flat like window glass. The glass, or *lens*, is curved in a special way that changes how we see by bending the light that comes into our eyes. On the chalkboard, draw diagrams of the two different kinds of lenses to explain that a *concave* lens makes things look farther away, while a *convex* lens makes things look closer.

At the bottom of a sheet of cardboard, cut out a semicircle an inch in diameter. Tape a comb over the cardboard so that the teeth of the comb cover the hole. Place a sheet of white paper on a table. Now ask a volunteer to hold the cardboard upright, semicircle down, on the table. Darken the room and have another volunteer hold a flashlight behind the cardboard so that the beam shines through the teeth of the comb and creates a pattern of parallel dark and light lines on the paper. (It may be necessary to lay the paper on top of one or two books to get the clearest pattern of light and shadow through the comb.)

Next place a magnifying glass, which is actually a convex lens, upright in front of the comb. Adjust the angle of the lens until the alternating beams of light and shadow from the comb's teeth converge. Explain that the convex lens bends light rays so that they move closer together.

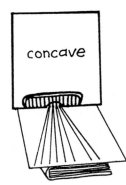

When you substitute a concave lens (from a pair of eyeglasses made to correct nearsightedness), the pattern of light and dark stripes will spread out. A concave lens bends light rays so they move farther apart.

Explain to children that the eyes of people who are near- or farsighted have lenses that do not focus light clearly on the back of the eye, or *retina*. Corrective lenses in eyeglasses bend the light entering the eye to focus it properly.

Up Periscope!

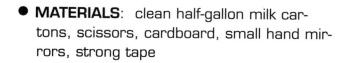

- **CONCEPT**: Light bounces from one reflective surface to another.

- **MATERIALS**: clean half-gallon milk cartons, scissors, cardboard, small hand mirrors, strong tape

- **PREPARATION**: Ask children to bring in clean milk cartons.

Intermediate-grade students can make periscopes on their own. Lower-grade teachers can make periscopes for children to experiment with.

Ask students if they know how sailors on a submarine below the surface of the water are able to see what is happening above the surface. They use a *periscope*. Tell children they can make periscopes and learn how they work. (For younger children, explain that you will make a periscope for them to try.)

Cut the tops off two half-gallon milk cartons. Cut two cardboard rectangles the same width as the milk cartons (3 3/4" x 5 1/4"). Use strong tape to fasten a small mirror, reflective side up, to the center of each cardboard rectangle. Then wedge a cardboard rectangle with the mirror facing up into each carton at roughly a 45° angle and fasten firmly in place with strong tape. Cut a window 1 1/2" square, near the bottom of each carton, from the side that faces the mirror. Turn one carton upside down, positioning the open ends of the two carton-halves together so that the windows are facing opposite sides. Fasten with tape and your periscope is ready!

Let students experiment looking through the bottom hole to see objects above or to the side of them. The illustration on this page shows some ways children might use their periscopes to see objects above or to the side.

Explore with children how periscopes work. Draw a diagram on the chalkboard to show how light hitting the upper mirror is reflected into the lower mirror and then to the eyes of the person looking through the periscope.

Weighing Work

- **CONCEPT**: A *spring scale* can measure amounts of work.

- **MATERIALS**: pipe cleaners, rubber bands, drinking straws cut into thirds, paper clips, 3" x 12" strips of cardboard, tape, 5" lengths of string

Distribute materials and give students the following instructions, demonstrating as you go along:

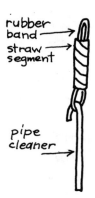

rubber band

straw segment

pipe cleaner

1. Hook one end of a pipe cleaner to a rubber band. Use the pipe cleaner to "thread" the rubber band through a straw segment.
2. Hook a paper clip to one end of the rubber band and slide the paper clip onto one end of a cardboard strip. Tape the straw firmly to the cardboard.

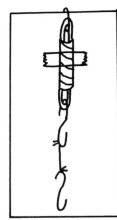

3. Open another paper clip to make an "S-hook." Remove the pipe cleaner and replace it with one end of the S-hook.
4. Tie one end of the string to the free end of the S-hook. Then open another paper clip to make another S-hook and tie it to the free end of the string.

Now try the following activity to see how this spring scale measures work.

Are You So Inclined?

- **CONCEPT**: An inclined plane is a simple machine that makes work easier.

- **MATERIALS**: a bag of marbles or other weights with a string attached, a spring scale, an inclined plane, a yardstick or meter stick

Tell students to hook the bag of weights to a spring scale and use the scale to pick up the bag, noticing how far the rubber band stretches. Then have children use the scale to pull the bag up the inclined plane. The rubber band will not stretch as far this time. Why?

Help students measure the distance from the floor to the high end of the inclined plane and compare it with the longer distance from one end of the plane to the other. Surprisingly, it takes less work to move a load over a longer distance than a shorter distance.

Name_____ Date_____

Longer Distance
Means Less Work

Measure the length of the inclined plane with a ruler. Then measure
the distance from the high end of the plane to the ground. Write
down your measurements. At the bottom of the page, tell why it takes
less work to lift a load on an inclined plane than to lift the same load
straight up.

The inclined plane measures _____ from A to B.

The distance from C to D measures_____ .

The inclined plane makes lifting a load easier because

_____

_____

© 1994 by Troll Associates, Inc.

Rolling Along on Ball Bearings

- **CONCEPT**: Rolling reduces friction.

- **MATERIALS**: jar lids, marbles

Divide the class into groups. Have each group put a jar lid, open side down, on a table and try to spin it. Ask students why the lid won't spin. Explain that *friction*, or rubbing, between the lid and the table kept the lid from turning. Suggest that students fit as many marbles as they can under the lid and try spinning it again. Why did the marbles make a difference? Explain that, by rolling, the marbles reduced the friction.

Wheels Need Axles

- **CONCEPT**: Wheels rotate on axles.

- **MATERIALS**: heavy books, marbles, skateboards or toy trucks, modeling clay, pencils

Let children work in groups. Ask the children to try pushing a book along the floor, then to put marbles under the book and try pushing it that way. The book moves more easily, but the marbles don't stay in place. Now let them push the book while it sits on a skateboard. Why do the wheels of a skateboard or a truck stay in place, when the marbles don't? Help children to see that unlike the marbles, the wheels of the skateboard or truck are attached to and revolve around *axles*.

Instruct children to roll clay into balls; these are like the marbles. How can they make them more like wheels? Have children experiment until they have flattened the balls into discs and stuck pencils through them. Now they have made wheels and axles. Explain that the wheel is a simple machine that makes it easier to move objects from one place to another.

Here's to Gears!

- **CONCEPT**: Gears make work easier.

- **MATERIALS**: an eggbeater, ridged bottle caps, a hammer, nails, small pieces of board (obtainable from a lumberyard)

- **PREPARATION**: These simple gear boards should be made by adults only. You will need a two-gear board and a three-gear board for each group of students. Nail bottle caps loosely to a wooden board, close enough so that the ridges on their rims mesh like gear teeth. The caps must be able to rotate freely. (See illustration below.)

Show students an old-fashioned eggbeater and let them try it out. Point out that turning the handle makes the blades turn. The blades rotate horizontally while the handle turns vertically. Help students notice that for each turn of the handle the blades turn several times.

Call children's attention to the *gears* on the eggbeater. Explain that *gears* are wheels with little teeth that mesh together. Ask students what turns the handle of the eggbeater. (someone's hand) What does the handle turn? (the first gear) What does the first gear turn? (the second gear) How are the two gears on the eggbeater different from each other? (The first gear is larger.) How many times does the smaller gear turn for each turn of the larger gear? How do gears make it easier to beat eggs?

Divide the class into groups and give each group a two-gear board and a three-gear board. Have a child in each group slowly turn the left-hand gear on the two-gear board in a clockwise direction. The other gear turns *counter*clockwise. Have students try the three-gear board. The two side gears turn in one direction, while the middle gear turns the opposite way. In which direction would a fourth gear turn? (Note that all the gears turn the same number of times because they are all the same size.)

Ask students to name other familiar ways in which gears are used—bicycles, clocks, can openers, hand drills, and so on. If possible, bring in examples for the class to examine.

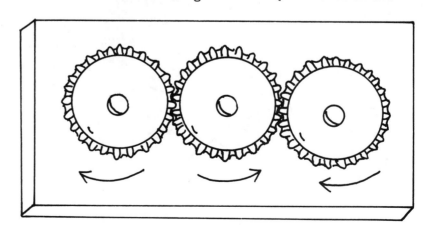

Screws and You

- **CONCEPT**: Screws fasten things together.

- **MATERIALS**: wood blocks, large screws, a hammer, large nails, a cake of soap, screwdrivers

- **PREPARATION**: Prepare a wood block and four screws for each group. Use a hammer and nail to make four holes in the block. Rub the threads of the four screws with soap to make them easier to turn. Drive a screw all the way into each hole, then screw each one out part way. (For younger children, either very large screws and screwdrivers or Phillips-head screws and screwdrivers will be easier to manipulate.)

Hold up a nail and a large wood screw. Let children examine them but not play with them—they are sharp. Encourage children to describe the differences they see between the screw and the nail. Note that the screw has a slotted head, in contrast to the flat head of the nail. Point out that the nail is smooth, but the screw has spiral ridges, known as *threads*. Arrange children in groups and provide each with a prepared wood block and a screwdriver. Let group members take turns screwing and unscrewing the screws.

Can children pull or push the screws in or out without the screwdrivers? Why do children think screws are good for fastening and holding objects together?

Have children name some familiar ways in which screws are used. Point out that the threaded base of an incandescent light bulb is really a screw that holds the bulb in its socket. How about threaded bottle and jar caps or the tops of toothpaste tubes?

Building Up Your Pull with Pulleys

- **CONCEPT**: Pulleys can change the direction of applied energy or lessen the amount of force needed to move a weight.

- **MATERIALS**: a yardstick, two adhesive-backed hooks, two pulleys (available at hardware stores), 2 feet of string, a dozen marbles, a pail with a handle, a spring scale (obtainable from science catalogues or can be made according to the instructions on page 70), three S-hooks (available at hardware stores or can be made by opening paper clips)

- **PREPARATION**: Fasten two adhesive-backed hooks to the yardstick, as shown in the illustrations below.

Ask students if they have ever seen a flag being raised on a pole. Can they describe how it is done? Recall that someone at the base of the pole pulls *down* on a rope, and the flag moves *up* the pole. This is certainly a lot easier than if the person had to climb up the pole holding the flag!

Show students a pulley, explaining that this device makes it possible to raise a flag. Pulleys can also make it easier to lift a weight.

Have a child rest the yardstick across two desks so the hooks hang between the desks. Help a volunteer thread a string through a pulley and hang the pulley from a hook on the yardstick. Ask students to put the marbles in a pail and weigh the pail with the spring scale. Remove the pail from the scale and help a

volunteer tie an S-hook at one end of the string threaded through the pulley. Tie a loop in the other end. Hang the pail handle from the S-hook and hook the spring scale through the loop. Show a child how to raise the pail by pulling *down* on the spring scale. The weight on the scale should be roughly the same as when the pail was lifted.

IT'S EASIER.

Now rig a *movable* pulley, using the illustration below as a guide. This time when a child pulls on the scale to lift the pail, the weight shown will be less. (It should be exactly half, but friction between string and pulley will throw off the measurement slightly.) Using two pulleys decreased the energy needed to lift the pail.

Pushing Down to Lift Up

- **CONCEPT**: Levers help us lift weight.

- **MATERIALS**: a large carton of books, a sturdy block of wood, a board about 6 feet long

If a seesaw is readily available, use it to experiment with. If not, draw a seesaw on the chalkboard. Explain that the seesaw is really a machine called a *lever*. Can children tell what holds the seesaw up? Show children the center and explain that this support point is called the *fulcrum*.

Place a heavy carton of books on the floor and ask students to try to lift it. The carton should be heavy enough so it will be difficult, or even impossible, for them to lift. (Don't let children strain themselves.)

Now set up a lever in the classroom. Place a sturdy block of wood on the floor and rest the board on top of it, more or less at its midpoint. Slide the carton onto one end of the board and ask a child to lift the carton by pushing down on the opposite end of the board. Point out that the box is a good deal easier to lift pushing *down* than it was lifting *up* because we are working with gravity rather than against it.

Inform children that lifting can be easier still, because a lever can provide what scientists call a *mechanical advantage*—that is, it can actually decrease the amount of energy needed to lift the weight of the box. Demonstrate by removing the carton from the board and shifting the board so that the fulcrum is much closer to one end. Slide the carton onto the short end, and ask volunteers to try lifting the carton by pushing down on the long end. They should find the box even easier to lift.

Help students conclude that the longer the length of the end that is pushed (the *effort arm*) compared with the length of the end that lifts the weight (the *load arm*), the greater the *mechanical advantage* will be.

You might mention that Archimedes, the great scientist of ancient Greece, declared that with a lever long enough and a place to stand, he could move the whole world! In principle he was right!

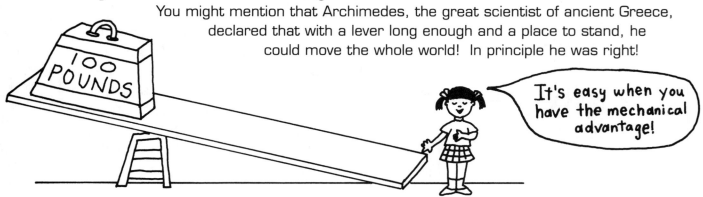

It's easy when you have the mechanical advantage!

Which Liquid Has More Pull?

- **CONCEPT**: Molecules of the same substance attract each other.

- **MATERIALS**: flat-bottomed clear plastic glasses, water, food coloring, rubbing alcohol, aluminum foil, eyedroppers

- **PREPARATION**: Mix food coloring into enough water to supply a little colored water to each group of children.

Tell students that they are going to be *chemists*. Explain that one thing chemists do is mix different liquids together to see how they will react.

Divide the class into groups and give each group a glass with a little colored water (barely enough to cover the bottom of the glass), a glass with a little alcohol, a piece of foil, and an eyedropper. Have children place the glasses of water on foil so they can see more easily what happens in the glass. (Remind students that the alcohol should not be tasted or swallowed.)

Tell children to watch the bottom of the glass carefully as a child uses the eye-

dropper to drip alcohol into the water. What do children observe? They should see that the colored water will immediately move away from the alcohol, making a ring of colored liquid around an island of clear liquid. Where the two liquids meet there will be a lot of movement, or *pulsation*. Eventually, the two liquids will mix together making a single solution of a uniform color.

Explain that a *molecule* is a very small particle of a substance. It is too small to see. Molecules of the same liquid *attract*, or pull each other together. When the alcohol was added to the water, the water molecules pulled toward each other and the alcohol molecules did the same. Because the molecules pulled toward each other, each liquid pulled *away* from the other liquid.

Go on to explain that water molecules have a stronger pull than alcohol molecules, so as they moved toward the outer edge of the glass, they pulled the alcohol molecules along. That's why the tiny amount of alcohol spread out so much. Then the water molecules began to pull in the alcohol molecules, causing the pulsating movement the students saw. Eventually, the alcohol and water mixed together completely.

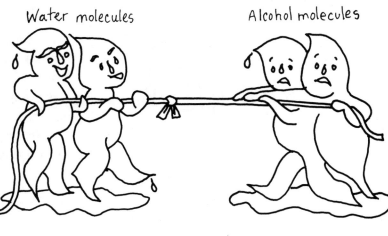

Water molecules   Alcohol molecules

Layers in a Glass

- **CONCEPT**: Low-density liquids float on those of higher density.

- **MATERIALS**: water, a tall clear jar, food coloring (two colors), rubbing alcohol, a cup or glass, cooking oil

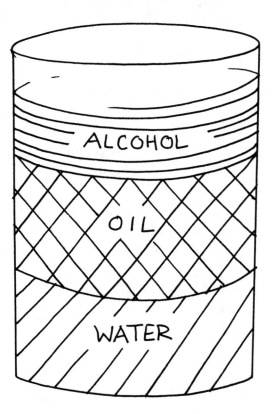

Students will learn more about liquids by observing what happens—or doesn't happen—when liquids are mixed together.

Have students prepare the set-up for this experiment. Ask one child to pour 2 inches of water into a jar and mix in some food coloring. Have another child add a different color to an inch or two of alcohol in a cup or glass. Help a third student pour some oil slowly and carefully down the inside wall of the jar into the water. The oil will not mix with the water but will form a separate layer on top, made visible by the food coloring in the water. Do students have any idea why this happened? Explain that the oil and water molecules pull away from each other so that the two liquids will not mix. The oil floats on top because it is lighter than water.

Next have a student carefully add the colored alcohol, which will form another layer on top of the oil. Challenge students to suggest an explanation. (Alcohol, like water, doesn't mix with oil; alcohol is lighter than oil.)

For students who would like to experiment further, challenge them to see what happens when they mix oil and water in different ways. Suggest pouring oil into a container first and then adding water. (The water, being heavier, will sink to the bottom, but the two liquids will not mix.) What if they put oil and water in a closed jar and shake? (The two liquids will mix and then separate. The oil will remain on top.) Explain to more advanced students that chemists call liquids that will not mix together *immiscible liquids*. (Remind students not to taste or swallow substances with which they are experimenting.)

Chemistry Heats Things Up

- **CONCEPT**: Rusting (oxidation) is a chemical reaction that produces heat.

- **MATERIALS**: plain steel-wool pads, scissors, jars with lids, room thermometers (small enough to fit in a jar when closed), vinegar, small bowls or saucers

- **PREPARATION**: Cut enough steel-wool pads in half to supply half a pad to each group of students.

Divide the class into groups and distribute materials. Assign one child in each group to be responsible for timing the different phases of the activity, using the classroom clock or a watch with a second hand.

Tell the groups that they will conduct a chemistry experiment that will produce heat. Before they begin, have children place the thermometers in the jars and close the lids. After five minutes, have them note the temperatures and write down their readings. Why do students think scientists need to record such information? Explain that in order to see if the inside of the jar is heated by the chemical reaction, they need to know the temperature inside the jar at the start of the experiment.

Ask students to pour a little vinegar into the bowls or saucers, soak the steel-wool pads in the vinegar for two minutes, remove them, and carefully squeeze out the excess vinegar. Next have students remove the thermometers from the jars, wrap the soaked steel wool around the bulb of each thermometer, place the thermometers back in the jars, and screw on the lids. Leave the wrapped thermometers in the jars for about fifteen minutes, then remove the thermometers and record the temperatures. The readings on the thermometers should be noticeably higher (about three or four degrees).

Before challenging students to explain what happened, ask if they've ever seen metal that has rusted. Does rusted metal *look* different? Explain that *rusting* is a chemical reaction between metal molecules and the oxygen in the air. The scientific term for this reaction is *oxidation*. Oxidation, like most chemical reactions, uses up energy, which is released in the form of heat. Go on to explain that the vinegar makes metal rust very quickly. Put this information together to explain the rise in temperature.

Moving Molecules

- **CONCEPT**: Matter is made of molecules that are always in motion.

- **MATERIALS**: water, clear plastic glasses, food coloring

Give students glasses of water and tell them to let the water become still. Do they think the water is moving? Help students to find out if the water is really moving or not.

Have children add a drop of food coloring to the glasses. What makes the color spread if the water isn't moving? Explain that water molecules (as all molecules) are always in motion, even when they look like they're standing still. The molecules in solid objects move more slowly; the molecules in gases, such as air, move fastest of all.

Funny Money

- **CONCEPT**: Acetic acid reacts with copper to form a green compound.

- **MATERIALS**: a paper towel, a saucer, vinegar, pennies

Inform the class that chemists often learn about different substances by observing if a chemical reaction results in a color change.

Ask a student to fold a paper towel into a square and lay it on a saucer. Have another child pour enough vinegar into the saucer to wet the towel thoroughly. Tell a third child to place a few pennies on the towel and leave them for a full day or until the tops of the coins turn green. Why do children think this happens? Explain that vinegar (*acetic acid*) reacts with the copper pennies to form *copper acetate*, the green compound that coated the pennies.

What conclusions can students draw from this experiment? Can they test whether a metal object contains copper? Have they found a way to test whether a liquid contains acetic acid?

Cabbage Chemistry

- **CONCEPT**: Cabbage juice indicates the presence of an acid or a base.

- **MATERIALS**: half a raw red cabbage, a grater, a bowl, hot water, a measuring cup, a jar with a lid, a strainer, small paper cups, eyedroppers, lemon juice, water, baking soda, strong tea, milk, orange juice, soapy water, ginger ale, saucers

- **PREPARATION**: Cut the half cabbage in two and grate it into a bowl. Pour a cupful of hot water over the shredded cabbage, pack the cabbage down with your hand, and let it stand for three hours. The chemicals that color the cabbage will dissolve, turning the water purple. Strain the purple liquid into a jar, discard the cabbage, and *refrigerate the liquid when not in use.*

Inform the class that some liquids, when mixed together, change color. These color changes help chemists learn more about the content of different liquids. They call the solution that changes color the *indicator*. Announce that the class is going to experiment with a purple indicator made from cabbage. Divide the class into groups and give each group small cups of cabbage juice, lemon juice, and plain water; an eyedropper; and a spoonful of baking soda. Also provide each group with a light-colored saucer.

Have one member of each group drip a few drops of cabbage juice onto the saucer. Have a second child add a few drops of lemon juice. The indicator will turn red! Explain that lemon juice contains *citric acid*, and that a chemical in cabbage juice reacts with the acid to turn it red. (You might explain that most liquids that taste sour are acids, but chemists can't test liquids by tasting them—some liquids are poisonous!)

Have the groups wash out their saucers and tell them to mix the baking soda with plain water. Instruct them to drip a little more cabbage juice onto the saucer, followed by a little of the baking-soda solution. This time the indicator will turn green! Baking soda (*sodium bicarbonate*) is a *base* (the opposite of an acid).

Let the groups experiment with other liquids to see whether they are acids or bases. Plain water will not change the color of the indicator at all because it is neither an acid nor a base, but *neutral*.

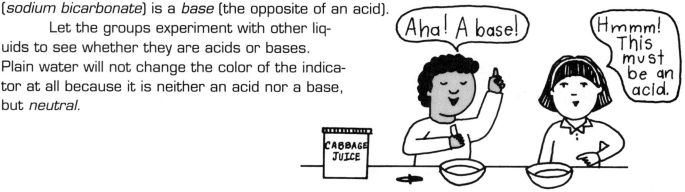

Name_____ Date_____

Acid or Base?

Use cabbage juice as an indicator to discover which of the following liquids are acids and which are bases. Write your results below.

	Color of the Indicator	Acid or Base
Strong tea		
Milk		
Orange juice		
Soapy water		
Ginger ale		

© 1994 by Troll Associates, Inc.

An Acid Test

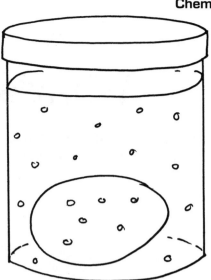

- **CONCEPT**: An eggshell will dissolve in acid.

- **MATERIALS**: a raw egg, a one-pint clear glass jar with a lid, a pint of clear vinegar

Help a child place an egg in a jar without cracking the shell. Ask a volunteer to pour in the vinegar and cover the jar. Have students examine the egg right away and again periodically during the next twenty-four hours. They should see bubbles appear instantly on the shell, increasing over time. Within a day, they will find the egg stripped of its shell, pieces of which may be floating on the surface. What do children think happened to the shell? Explain that vinegar is a strong acid (*acetic acid*). The eggshell is made of *calcium carbonate*, which dissolves in acid. The reaction produces bubbles of carbon dioxide.

Secret Messages

- **CONCEPT**: Invisible ink can be made from vinegar or lemon juice.

- **MATERIALS**: narrow paintbrushes, vinegar or lemon juice in a saucer, blank paper, an unshaded lamp

Divide students into groups and tell them that they are going to write secret messages with invisible ink. Instruct them to dip paintbrushes in vinegar or lemon juice and write their messages. The messages will be invisible. Have the groups trade messages and hold each message over a lighted incandescent bulb. The heat of the bulb makes the secret writing appear! Tell children that a chemical reaction between the juice or vinegar and the paper lowered the *ignition point* of the paper, allowing mild heat to singe it. The paper untouched by the acid will not burn unless exposed to more intense heat.

Name_____ Date_____

What's the Picture?

Use invisible ink to connect the dots below. Then hold the paper over a lighted bulb to see what you've drawn.

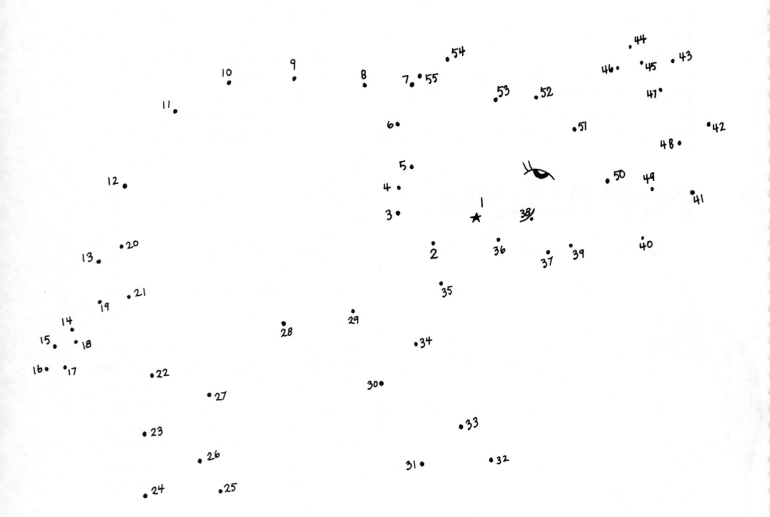

© 1994 by Troll Associates, Inc.

Magnets Are Choosy

- **CONCEPT**: Magnets attract some things but not others.

- **MATERIALS**: magnets, sticks, 12" lengths of string, open shoe boxes, various small items (paper clips, erasers, chalk, crayons, aluminum foil, screws, bolts, pieces of paper, cardboard, wood, glass, etc.)

- **PREPARATION**: Make magnetic "fishing rods" by tying a magnet to the end of each stick with a string.

Divide the class into groups and give each group a magnetic fishing rod, an open shoe box, and some small items such as those listed above. Have children take turns placing things in the boxes and trying to "fish" them out with the magnets. Suggest that they keep lists of which items the magnets attract and which ones they do not. Afterward, compare the lists and see if the class can draw conclusions about what magnets do and do not attract.

A Field of Filings

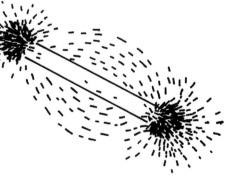

- **CONCEPT**: A magnet's strongest parts are its poles.

- **MATERIALS**: a bar magnet, a sheet of white paper, a zip-lock bag filled with iron filings

Don't let children handle the iron filings at any time. Always keep the filings in the zip-lock bag. Trace the outline of a bar magnet on a sheet of paper and place the magnet on a table with the outline over it. Shake the plastic bag to disperse the filings throughout the bag. Ask a child to place the bag over the outline of the magnet and tap the bag lightly. What happens? Children should see the filings form into a pattern similar to the one in the illustration above, showing the magnet's *lines of force*. Explain that the filings cluster around the ends of the magnet because these ends are the *poles*, or the strongest parts.

Name_____ Date_____

Match Up the Magnets

Look at the three patterns of iron filings. Can you tell which magnet
made each one? Draw lines to connect each pattern with the correct
magnet.

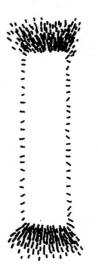 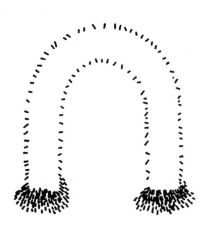 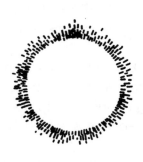

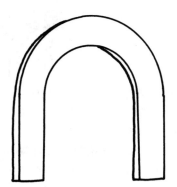  

© 1994 by Troll Associates, Inc.

Poles Together, Poles Apart

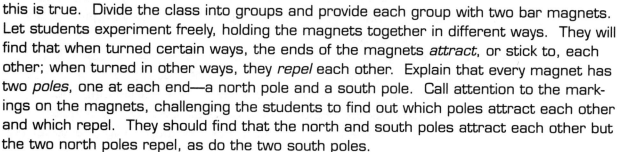

- **CONCEPT**: Like poles of a magnet repel; opposite poles attract.

- **MATERIALS**: bar magnets with poles marked N(orth) and S(outh)

Ask children if they've ever heard the saying "Opposites attract." Have them experiment to see if this is true. Divide the class into groups and provide each group with two bar magnets. Let students experiment freely, holding the magnets together in different ways. They will find that when turned certain ways, the ends of the magnets *attract*, or stick to, each other; when turned in other ways, they *repel* each other. Explain that every magnet has two *poles*, one at each end—a north pole and a south pole. Call attention to the markings on the magnets, challenging the students to find out which poles attract each other and which repel. They should find that the north and south poles attract each other but the two north poles repel, as do the two south poles.

The Giant Magnet

- **CONCEPT**: The earth is a magnet.

- **MATERIALS**: paper, a compass, a bar magnet, thread

Instruct a student to write "NORTH" and "SOUTH" on opposite ends of a piece of paper. Have another student use the compass to orient the paper so the end marked NORTH actually points north. Tie a thread around the middle of a bar magnet and dangle it over the paper. As children watch, they should see the magnet line up with the north pole pointing north and with the south pole pointing south. Explain that the entire earth is a magnet with its own north and south poles.

Students might wonder why the north pole of the earth attracts the north pole of the magnet, when they've learned that like poles repel each other. Scientifically speaking, what we call the north pole of a magnet is *not* really its north pole, but its *north-seeking* pole.

Are All Magnets Created Equal?

- **CONCEPT**: Some magnets are stronger than others.

- **MATERIALS**: magnets of several types and sizes, paper clips, a marker

Give each group of students several different kinds of magnets. Ask the children if they think all magnets are equally strong. Can they suggest a way to find out?

Demonstrate how to hang paper clips in a chain from a magnet as shown in the illustration. Instruct groups to make chains with their magnets, adding a clip at a time until the chains break. Suggest they number their magnets with a marker and record how many clips each magnet can hold before the chain breaks. Discuss the results, leading the children to conclude that the maximum lengths of the paper-clip chains varied among the different magnets because not all magnets are equally strong.

Breaking the Cardboard Barrier!

- **CONCEPT**: Magnets attract through nonmagnetic materials.

- **MATERIALS**: sheets of cardboard, magnets, paper clips

Show the class a sheet of cardboard and a magnet. Will the magnet attract the cardboard? Have a student test to find out. Then have another student demonstrate that magnets do attract paper clips. Ask children if they think a magnet will attract paper clips *through* the cardboard. How can children find out?

Distribute the materials to groups. Show the groups how to place a piece of cardboard like a bridge between two stacks of books. Have children lay paper clips on the cardboard and try to move the clips by moving magnets across the bottom surface of the cardboard. What does this experiment show? Lead children to deduce that magnets are effective through a nonmagnetic substance.

Creating Craters

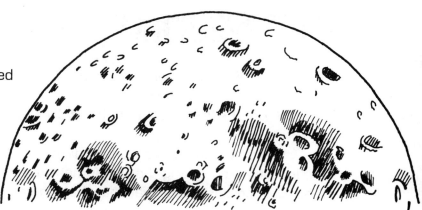

- **CONCEPT**: Craters are caused by the impact of objects from space.

- **MATERIALS**: buckets, soil, spades, water, mixing spoons, pie pans

This activity is best done outdoors, because it involves working with mud and can be messy.

Ask children if they know what is Earth's closest neighbor in space. (the moon) Discuss what children know about the moon, mentioning that the moon has virtually no atmosphere. Ask whether students have seen close-up pictures of the moon in a book or at a planetarium. Display photographs of the lunar surface for children to examine, pointing out that the dark circular patterns they see on the moon's surface are really huge holes called *craters*. Can students guess how the craters were formed? Involve the class in the following activity to show how.

THE MOON

Take the class outside and have students fill buckets with soil. Tell them to mix water with the soil until the resulting mud has the consistency of thick pudding. Have children fill the pie pans with mud, and smooth the surfaces as much as possible.

Now let children take turns spooning up mud from the buckets and dropping the contents of the spoons onto the mud in the pans. When all the surfaces are cratered, set aside the pans to dry. Within a few days the contents of the pie pans will give a rough approximation of the lunar surface.

Explain that over many years, meteors, asteroids, and other objects flying through space have smashed into the moon, creating craters at the points of impact. Tell the class that there are craters on the earth too, formed in the same way. But the earth's atmosphere creates friction, which slows an object down and generates such intense heat that virtually all of the object is burned up before it reaches the earth's surface. Because of the moon's lack of atmosphere, asteroids strike the surface at almost full speed. (Make sure children understand that the moon's surface is solid and dry—not muddy.)

Safe Sunshine

- **CONCEPT**: There is a safe way to observe the sun.

- **MATERIALS**: a pair of binoculars, a mirror

Warn students *never* to look directly at the sun; its light is so strong that it can harm their eyes. But there is a safe way that the sun can be viewed. On a sunny day, place a pair of binoculars in a window, aiming straight at the sun. Suggest that students prop the binoculars in place by using books to steady them as shown in the illustration. Hold a mirror at an angle in front of one of the eyepieces and adjust it to reflect an image of the sun on a blank wall several feet away. Ask a child to darken the room as much as possible. If the binoculars are very good, children will even be able see the dark areas called *sunspots* on the sun's surface. If birds or clouds cross the sun, children will see them, too.

Big Shadows, Little Shadows

- **CONCEPT**: The length of shadows changes as the sun moves.

- **MATERIALS**: flashlights, milk cartons

Encourage children to talk about shadows. What are they? How are they formed? How do they move? Do shadows always look the same, or do they change?

Divide the class into groups and pass out materials. Have a child in each group shine the flashlight on the milk carton from almost directly above it. Ask how the size and shape of the shadow compare to the actual carton. Tell the child to move the flashlight as if it were the sun crossing the sky, keeping it aimed at the carton. What happens to the shadow? The sun moving across the sky makes our shadows change in length just as the flashlight changed the shadow of the carton.

Name_____ Date_____

Where's the Sun?

Look at the three children below. Notice the length of their shadows.
In which directions are the shadows pointing? For each child, draw
the sun where it would be in order to cast that kind of shadow.

© 1994 by Troll Associates, Inc.

What Turns on the Moonlight?

- **CONCEPT**: Moonlight is the reflected light of the sun.

- **MATERIALS**: a flashlight, a mirror

Ask students why we don't feel warmth from the moon at night as we do from the sun during the daytime. Guide the discussion by asking what makes sunlight. Does the moon produce its own light, like the sun? This demonstration will give them a clue.

Have one child hold a mirror in front of the room. Ask another child to hold a flashlight in back of the class. Darken the room and have the child with the light shine it on the mirror. What makes the mirror bright? If the moon acts like a mirror, then what is the source of the light it reflects? Lead the children to conclude that the moon reflects light from the sun as the mirror reflects the beam of the flashlight.

What Outshines the Moon?

- **CONCEPT**: The moon may be overhead in the daytime, even though we cannot see it.

- **MATERIALS**: a flashlight, black construction paper, tape

This demonstration works best on a sunny day. Ask the class why we don't see the moon during the day. Does it go away? Have students close the shades or blinds while others tape black construction paper to a wall. Hand a child a flashlight and ask him or her to stand across the room from the construction paper. Darken the room and have the child shine the light on the paper. While it is on, turn on the lights and have the shades or blinds opened. What happens to the light on the paper? Can the children now explain why the moon isn't usually seen in the daytime? Help them conclude that the sun's light is too strong for the relatively dim reflected light of the moon to be seen.

Tilting Toward the Sun

● **CONCEPT**: The tilt of the earth's axis causes six-month days and nights at the poles.

● **MATERIALS**: a globe, a strong flashlight

Share ideas about why we have day and night. Demonstrate by shining a flashlight (the "sun") on a globe (the "earth") and rotating the globe to show that the earth's *rotation* causes alternate periods of light and darkness.

Inquire of children if they have ever heard the expression "land of the midnight sun." What do children think the expression means? Tell them that parts of the earth, such as northernmost Scandinavia, lie close to the North Pole and point out those areas on a globe. Explain that the regions of the earth that are closest to the North Pole—and the South Pole, too—have days and nights that are *six months long!* Invite children to imagine what it would be like to live in such a place.

Point out that the globe, like the real earth, rotates on a tilted axis. Have students place the globe at one end of the table with the North Pole tilted toward the opposite end. Have a child represent the sun by standing at the opposite end of the table. Tell the "sun" to shine a strong flashlight on the globe, aiming the light at the equator. Darken the room and ask a student to turn the globe slowly. Most of the globe goes from "daytime" to "nighttime" with each revolution, but the North Pole stays lit all the time and the South Pole stays dark. Remind the class that the earth rotates around the sun taking one year to complete an orbit. How far will the earth go in half a year? Have the "sun" and the globe switch places to represent the earth's half-year orbit around the sun.

Now the South Pole will be tilted toward the "sun" (see illustration). This means that the South Pole will remain in the light when the globe is turned, but the North Pole will stay dark.

The Temperature's Greater at the Equator

- **CONCEPT**: Direct sunlight gives off more heat than angled sunlight.

- **MATERIALS**: a globe, black construction paper, tape, a flashlight

Invite children to recall the hottest weather they ever experienced. What about the coldest? At the North and South Poles it stays so cold that both poles are covered with thick layers of ice that *never* melt! The cold is too harsh for people to live there.

Ask students to point out the poles on a globe and then find the equator. Tell them that this center region of the earth tends to have the hottest climate on the planet.

Make a cylindrical tube from black construction paper and secure it with tape. The tube should be wide enough to just fit over the bulb end of a flashlight. Tape the tube to the end of the flashlight. Have one child hold a sheet of black construction paper upright on a table, facing the class, while another student aims the light at the middle of the paper from several feet away.

Darken the room and ask children to watch the area of the paper lit by the beam. While the light shines straight ahead, the lit area is small and bright. Instruct the student holding the construction paper to slowly tilt the top of the paper away from the class, changing the angle at which the light hits it. Once the paper is tilted back several inches, ask students how the lit area changes. (The light now covers a larger area but is not as bright.)

Help students understand that direct beams of light are brighter than beams that strike a surface at an angle. Point out that the area that receives the most direct light from the sun is the equator, while the sun's light is most angled where it strikes the North and South Poles.

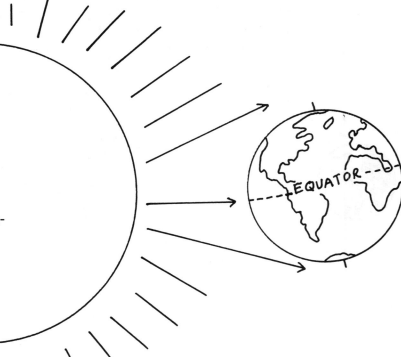

Different Angles

- **CONCEPT**: The tilt of the earth's axis causes seasonal changes.

- **MATERIALS**: a globe, an unshaded table lamp

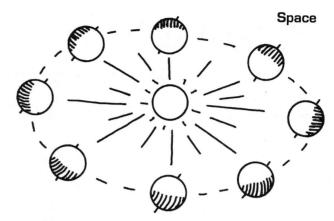

Ask the class how the four seasons differ in your area. How does the weather change? Do the plants change? What about the number of daylight hours? Brainstorm with students as to why we have seasons.

Place an unshaded lamp representing the sun in the middle of a table. With the students' help, locate your area on the globe. Position the globe on the table so that your area is tilted directly toward the "sun." Without changing the tilt of the axis, move the globe one quarter of the way around the "sun." Rotate the globe so that your area is still facing the light. Can students see that your area is now receiving less direct light? As you continue moving the globe around the "sun," remind the class that the earth makes one complete revolution around the sun per year. Challenge students to tell which position represents winter. (when your area is tilted away from the lamp)

What We'd Weigh on Other Worlds

- **CONCEPT**: Our weights would change on different planets.

- **MATERIALS**: a scale, calculators

Tell the class that astronauts on the moon could leap great distances because the moon's gravity is a fraction of the earth's. Inform children that gravity varies from planet to planet. Let them work out what they would weigh on other worlds. Have students take turns weighing themselves and recording their weights. Write on the chalkboard the names and relative gravities of the planets (see the chart on this page). Instruct students to multiply their weights by each planet's relative gravity. (Calculators are allowed!) For example, to learn what they would weigh on Venus, they'd multiply their weights by .90. On which planet would they weigh the most? On which would they weigh the least?

Mercury	.38
Venus	.90
Mars	.38
Jupiter	2.87
Saturn	1.32
Uranus	.93
Neptune	1.23
Pluto	.0022

Bibliography

You'll find the following Troll books useful in your science teaching:

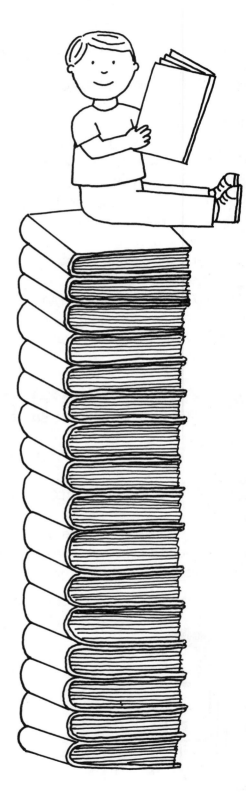

Plants
Damon, Laura *Wonders of Plants and Flowers*
Kuchalla, Susan *All About Seeds*
Marcus, Elizabeth *Amazing World of Plants*

Animals
Caitlin, Stephen *Amazing World of Birds*
Craig, Janet *Discovering Whales and Dolphins*
Jefferies, Lawrence *Amazing World of Animals*

The Human Body
Richardson, James *Science Dictionary of the Human Body*
Saunderson, Jane *Heart and Lungs*
Saunderson, Jane *Muscles and Bones*

The Senses
Jedrosz, Aleksander *Eyes*
Mathers, Douglas *Ears*
Smith, Kathie Billingslea *Tasting*
Smith, Kathie Billingslea *Touching*

The Environment
Craig, Janet *Wonders of the Rain Forest*
O'Neill, Mary *Nature in Danger*
Sanders, John *All About Deserts*

The Earth
Curran, Eileen *Mountains and Volcanoes*
Malin, Stuart *Story of the Earth*
Marcus, Elizabeth *Rocks and Minerals*

The Ocean
Adler, David *Our Amazing Ocean*
Craig, Janet *What's Under the Ocean*
Sabin, Louis *Wonders of the Sea*

Air and Water
Dickinson, Jane *Wonders of Water*
Jefferies, Lawrence *Air, Air, Air*

Weather
Adler, David *World of Weather*
Lambert, David *Weather*

Magnets
Adler, David *Amazing Magnets*

Space
Adams, Richard *Our Wonderful Solar System*
Adler, David *All About the Moon*
Hughes, Dr. David *Story of the Universe*
Wandelmaier, Roy *Stars*